INTRODUCING THE WORLD COUNCIL OF CHURCHES

Marlin VanElderen
& Martin Conway

Revised and enlarged edition

Risk
BOOK SERIES

WCC Publications, Geneva

Photos: WCC/Peter Williams unless otherwise indicated

Cover design: Rob Lucas

ISBN 2-8254-1353-4

© 2001, WCC Publications, the publishing division of the
World Council of Churches
150 route de Ferney, P.O. Box 2100
1211 Geneva 2, Switzerland
Website: http://www.wcc-coe.org

No. 96 in the Risk Book Series

Printed in Switzerland

Contents

Foreword

The first edition of this introduction to the contemporary ecumenical movement and to the World Council of Churches was published in 1990, prior to the Canberra assembly of the WCC. As Emilio Castro, general secretary at the time of the publication, said in his original foreword: "A large percentage of participants at our assemblies and consultations and even members of our committees and commissions are relative newcomers on the global ecumenical scene. At a time without ready access to ecumenical memory, this book helps fill an important gap."

Meanwhile another assembly has taken place at Harare in 1998 and the World Council of Churches has moved on. In an important policy document entitled "Towards a Common Understanding and Vision of the World Council of Churches", accepted by the Harare assembly, the Council has tried to clarify its role and place in the present ecumenical situation worldwide. Structures and programme emphases have changed and it proved necessary to prepare a revised edition of this introduction.

The first edition was written by Marlin VanElderen, then editor of the WCC's monthly magazine *One World* and later executive editor of the Council. His text was designed both for the general, interested reader and for students of ecumenism. He was also the coordinating editor of a volume covering the history of the ecumenical movement from 1968 up to the Harare assembly. After Marlin VanElderen's untimely death in June 2000, Martin Conway agreed to undertake the task of updating this more popular introduction. As a former staff member of the WCC and a long-time friend of the Council, he was well placed to assume this responsibility. We are very grateful to him for his careful work which has been carried out with commitment and honesty, respectfully keeping to much of the original text and format.

After explaining what the WCC is and does, the book gives a brief overview of the history of the ecumenical movement. Detailed chapters follow on the Council's life of acting and thinking together in faith. The final chapter is a frank assessment of the WCC's place and mission in today's world.

The bibliography has also been updated to include many recent publications of interest to those seeking to know more about the ecumenical movement.

It is hoped that this publication – which deals also with outside criticism of the Council's work – will reach a wide audience and will help many to understand better the Council's mission and raison d'être.

KONRAD RAISER
General Secretary
of the World Council of Churches

1. A Fellowship of Churches

Six views of the same Council

What is the World Council of Churches (WCC)? Ask that of a number of people who have had something to do with the Council, and their answers may well differ widely. That diversity of response no doubt witnesses to the vitality of what the churches have been doing together in this organization for more than fifty years. But it also points to a complexity that sometimes makes it hard for people to grasp just what the WCC is and is for.

• The WCC, some will say, is an organisation that responds with compassion and effective action when people are suffering.

Yes, when a devastating earthquake strikes somewhere around the world, the WCC – now in Action of Churches Together, a partnership with the Lutheran World Federation – acts immediately to learn what it can about the disaster and the needs and possibilities for church assistance. Then it appeals to church agencies in several countries for resources – food and blankets in some cases, money in almost all, experts who can bring short-term help in others. As such aid becomes available, the Council works with the local Christian groups in the stricken area to channel it to those who need it the most urgently and then to begin planning with the same groups for rehabilitation and reconstruction efforts that will go on long after the disaster has disappeared from the headlines.

• Others will speak of the WCC bringing together theologians, church leaders and other thoughtful Christians to explore the doctrinal issues on which their different traditions agree and disagree.

The Council's best-known work of this kind is the study document *Baptism, Eucharist and Ministry,* published in 1982. For centuries churches have rejected one another's teachings on these issues. Christian fellowship has been broken over whether baptism is appropriate for infants, or only for grown believers, over how Christ is present in the Lord's supper, over whether women may be ordained. Years of discussion within the WCC have not resolved these differences, but have enabled theological leaders from many traditions to present a common statement that can take all churches a long way towards mutual acceptance of each others' practices.

• Those who seek to live out the call in the gospel Jesus proclaimed by loving their neighbours as themselves know how much human suffering is rooted in injustice. So, many will point to the WCC's engagement on behalf of the "sinned-against" in the struggle against injustice as the heart of what the WCC is all about.

This engagement may take the form of "empowering" through moral or financial support, organizations of people who are oppressed because of their race. It may involve expert analysis and prophetic exposure of social, economic and political powers deforming the lives of millions. It may be expressed in encouraging small and marginalized communities, seldom if ever in the public eye, to take charge of their own future.

• In the foothills of the Jura mountain range, half an hour's drive from the WCC headquarters in Geneva, stands the Council's Ecumenical Institute, Bossey. Here the WCC takes shape as a centre of study and prayer, a means of inspiring and enabling people to work for Christian unity in their own contexts.

Hundreds of people come to Bossey each year for conferences and courses – ranging in length from a week to several months – which expand their understanding of what churches around the world are doing for and with one another. The life of the WCC is inspired by Jesus' prayer shortly before he was crucified, "May they all may be one... so that the world may believe that you sent me." The Council's initiatives to bring Christians together in service to the human family are echoed in the experience of living and working together as Christians from different backgrounds in places like Bossey.

• Many people would point to the patient and constructive efforts of the WCC to hold up the relevance of the church's message of peace and reconciliation in face of the conflicts that constantly tear our world apart.

For example, in the last stages of the 20th century the WCC on numerous occasions brought together church leaders from North and South Korea, to talk and pray together about their concern for the reunification of their country. Gradually they dared to ask each other how they – as Christians sharing the same language and culture though divided by a cruelly impermeable boundary – could work to break down the walls of hostility and fear. This initiative by the Korean churches, supported through the WCC by their brother and sister Christians around the world, injected the key element of hope into a situation previously judged hopeless.

• Many people will stress the importance of having a truly global constituency: one of the central values of the World Council of Churches is that churches from any and every part of the world can come together as equals.

Especially in Asia and the Middle East, yet increasingly in other areas also, members of Christian churches live amidst communities of other faith traditions and commitments, not always in peace and harmony. While it is good that Christians can know themselves involved in a worldwide fellowship, it is also a key dimension of the WCC's service to encourage believers of all traditions to respect and learn from their neighbours' faith and life.

A common basis

Each of these differing answers to the simple question: "What is the World Council of Churches?" highlights a different facet of the Council's commitment. It is understandable that not everyone will emphasize the same thing. People become acquainted with the WCC in a variety of ways; they have diverse interests; they have their own ideas of what matters most.

Still more, the agenda of the World Council changes, as do the concerns and priorities of the member churches. Ten or twenty years ago there was little if any concern in most churches about things that seem of high importance today: AIDS, for instance, the climate change arising from the

Delegates at the WCC's eighth assembly in Harare, Zimbabwe (1998)
WCC/Chris Black

"greenhouse effect", the international debt crisis and the disputes about globalization, to mention only a few.

So the attempt to answer the question "What is the World Council of Churches?" can remind us of the ancient Indian fable of the blind people describing an elephant. Each of them had touched only one part of the animal – one the trunk, another a tusk, the third a leg. Their descriptions were of course remarkably different, with none bearing much resemblance to an actual elephant.

The point of that story is not just that their limited experiences caused each and all of them to give a misleading description. Even to add their various pictures together would not give an adequate description. Partial pictures may be misleading as well as incomplete.

What is it, then, that can hold together the variety within the WCC? The straightforward answer is given in the first article of its Constitution, its Basis:

> The World Council of Churches is a fellowship of churches which confess the Lord Jesus Christ as God and Saviour according to the scriptures and therefore seek to fulfil together their common calling to the glory of the one God, Father, Son and Holy Spirit.

This Basis is not a full "confession of faith" as compared with the historic creeds and doctrinal decrees. It is a brief expression of the faith and commitment in which the Council is rooted, and thus offers the essential clues for understanding the Council's life and witness.

A multiplicity of member churches

The Basis describes the World Council as "a fellowship of churches". It is only *churches* that can become members of the Council. And they choose representatives to vote in the bodies that govern it.

The WCC has no definition of what is and is not meant by a "church"; it accepts each church – subject to conditions mentioned below – as that church sees and defines itself. Many of its members are bodies of local parishes or congregations organized in a national "church", while the Salvation Army, for instance, is an international community that was accepted into membership as one worldwide "church". Often the different churches are described as "denominations", but not all of them accept this designation.

All accept however that the WCC is an *inter-denominational* movement, inviting and expecting all its members to take seriously the factors that divide them, and to work constructively with and on those. This is said in distinction from those *non-denominational* movements which aim to achieve a functional unity by overlooking the divisive issues. Member churches of the WCC must be ready to bring their differences into discussion in the fellowship; this sometimes makes for tensions, even conflicts, but it also ensures that the fellowship has to wrestle with those divisions and can grow from doing so.

Of course the Council will never suggest that Christian presence and witness are limited to those bodies which are (or might become) members of the WCC. All over the world Christians can be found meeting and working in a huge variety of groups and agencies – basic Christian communities, house churches, charismatic renewal fellowships, action groups addressing certain specific ethical or political issues, etc. By no means all of these would wish to consider themselves "a church", let alone "the church", although in many cases their members will be among those most actively living out the faith of the church.

To become a member of the World Council of Churches, a church must meet several criteria. It must have a "sustained independent life and organization", including the right to decide to apply for WCC membership without needing the permission of any other body or person. It must acknowledge that all member churches are interdependent, and must practise "constructive ecumenical relations" with other churches in its country and region. Member churches are normally expected to have at least 25,000 persons as members; smaller churches with at least 10,000 members may become "associate member churches" provided they fulfil all the other criteria.

A member church must also declare its agreement with the Basis, and thus signify its readiness to play its part in the fellowship of the Council, to participate in the life and work of the Council and to take up commitment to the one ecumenical movement as integral to the mission of the church. There is no fixed membership fee, but the rules list among the responsibilities of membership that churches "make an annual contribution to the general budget of the WCC... commensurate with [their] resources". One thousand Swiss francs is presently being considered the minimum annual contribution.

At its founding assembly in Amsterdam in 1948 representatives from 147 churches constituted the World Council. Since then the number has grown to more than 340, from over 100 countries.

Christ and the scriptures

To look into the inner meaning of WCC membership, two key phrases in the Basis can be explored:

• The churches in the Council "confess the Lord Jesus Christ as God and Saviour". These words express "the conviction that the Lord of the church is God-among-us who continues to gather his children and to build his church himself", as a 1950 statement from the WCC central committee put it. "Conversation, cooperation and common witness of the churches must be based on the common recognition that Christ is the divine Head of the Body."

The WCC has no "official theology" to elaborate on this and comparable central issues about itself. It respects the freedom of the member churches to interpret this and other affirmations in the Basis according to their own teachings. Within the churches criticism of this phrase have come from opposite angles. Some say that by itself the confession of "the Lord Jesus Christ as God and Saviour" – a phrase from the foundational charter of the YMCA in 1855 – is too slender a ground for Christian unity; the Basis should include other fundamental doctrinal affirmations as well. Others say that this testimony to the divinity of Christ does less than justice to his humanity.

Konrad Raiser, general secretary of the WCC at the turn of the century, suggests that the "clear witness of faith in view of uncertainties, confusions and distortions" which the "simple formula" in the Basis offers was especially important at the time the WCC was formed, in the wake of the devastation of the second world war and the new threat from nuclear weapons. Events since then, he says, have given the churches "a new appreciation of the humanity of Christ, his suffering and his solidarity with those who live at the margin of history... The incarnation, as a perspective "from above", and the cross as a perspective "from below", have to be affirmed together."

• The common confession of the Lord Jesus Christ as God and Saviour, the Basis goes on to say, is "according to the scriptures". This emphasis on the Bible as the standard for what the church believes and teaches has a long history in the Christian tradition, even if in the Reformation tradition it became identified as typically Protestant. Already in the New Testament, quotations from the Hebrew Scriptures show that the early church believed its faith and proclamation were to be tested by scripture. The principle of faithfulness to the scriptures – of both testaments – was then enshrined in the 4th-century creed of the councils of Nicea and Constantinople.

The years leading up to the founding of the WCC were marked by a "rediscovery of the Bible" (title of a book by Suzanne de Diétrich, one of the first to be published by the Council, in 1942, when it was still "in process of formation"). The first stirrings of concern for Christian unity in modern times arose in small groups of Christians meeting for Bible study and prayer. As the first assembly of the WCC put it, "many Christians have found the Bible as a living, contemporary book". This shared point of reference is reflected in the central place given to the Bible in all WCC meetings.

Of course there is among the member churches no little diversity of teaching about the precise role, authority and interpretation of the Bible. Yet already in 1954 the second assembly in Evanston, near Chicago, could say:

> We must all listen together in the midst of our disunity to our one Lord speaking to us through holy scriptures. This is a hard thing to do. We will struggle to comprehend the meaning and authority of holy scripture. Yet whenever we are prepared to undertake together the study of the word of God and are resolved to be obedient to what we are told, we are on the way

Suzanne de Diétrich and Bossey students in the 1970s
Photo Oikoumene

towards realizing the oneness of the church in Christ in the actual state of our dividedness on earth.

A helpful distinction was drawn by the WCC's world conference on Faith and Order in 1963, between "Tradition" (understood as the gospel itself "transmitted from generation to generation in and by the church"), and "traditions" (the many different ways in which the Tradition has been understood and transmitted in different confessions and cultures). To realize that scripture is embedded in Tradition and should not be set over against Tradition has made it possible to move beyond the classic debate over whether revelation is given through scripture alone or through scripture and/or Tradition.

Some Christians accent the Lordship of Christ as the central point of the scriptural message; others point to justification by faith, or to rebirth in the Holy Spirit; others again will identify God's liberating activity, shown in the Exodus and the cross and resurrection of Jesus, as yet more central. Encounter between these varying emphases can prove one of the most fruitful aspects of participation in the WCC, provided that all are willing to acknowledge the particularity of their own interpretation of the Bible, and to submit that to correction under the guidance of the Holy Spirit.

Within the WCC in recent years, many people have been helped by encountering two new points of view: one that has come from reading the Bible through the eyes of the poor and oppressed, the other the realization that when women read the Bible "with their own eyes" (as a 1981 WCC consultation in Sheffield put it) they are "often able to see what has escaped men for centuries and to identify with what men could not feel or recognize in the texts". In relation to the diversity of cultures, a 1995 WCC consultation on intercultural hermeneutics wrote:

> Even before the gospel is heard in a culture, the Spirit of God is at work in its stories, seeking opportunities through them to draw all things towards the reality of God's power and presence revealed in the gospel. In addressing a culture, the gospel engages its stories, illuminating some more deeply, reinterpret-

ing others, challenging or rejecting still others, always deepening the meaning and significance of the culture in its light.... When churches from different cultures encounter each other in real communion, the resulting experience of the fullness of Christ transcends the experience of any church by itself; and the mutual assistance and shared mission they render offer a sign of God's reconciling purpose for all humanity in a world where the powerful often suppress diversity by destroying the culture of the weaker.

Hans-Ruedi Weber, for many years the WCC's secretary for biblical studies, suggests that "if we talk *about* the Bible, then the Bible is divisive. If we let the Bible talk to us, in the discipline of corporate Bible study, it will be uniting. But it will be uniting by affirming and also correcting our diversities, leading to mutual respect. If we let the Bible speak to us as it is, and don't squeeze it into a dogmatic straitjacket, we will see that there were already differences in the Christian community at the time the Bible was written. This liberates us for our diversity."

Togetherness in the fellowship

The word "fellowship" in the WCC's self-understanding appears already in the first document to propose such a body, the letter from the Ecumenical Patriarchate in 1920. Addressing "all the churches of Christ everywhere", after liberation from centuries of oppression under the Ottoman empire and in the atmosphere of freedom and hope at the end of the first world war, this Orthodox church called for the creation of "a koinonia of churches" – the same word used in Greek for the "League of Nations" proposed by US President Woodrow Wilson, and a word which plays a key role in the New Testament. The choice of this word, whose meaning is still being explored by scholars, pointed already then to such texts as Acts 2:42 which speaks of the early church "being devoted to the apostles' teaching and koinonia", usually rendered in English as "fellowship" or "communion".

A statement on "the unity of the church as koinonia" by the WCC's seventh assembly in Canberra in 1991 describes the church as "the foretaste" of communion with God, who intends "to gather the whole of creation under the Lordship of Christ Jesus". The church's purpose is therefore "to unite people with Christ in the power of the Spirit, to manifest communion in prayer and action and thus to point to the fullness of communion with God, with humanity and with the whole creation in the glory of the kingdom". Divided churches can already recognize "a certain degree of communion", the statement says, as they "walk together in mutual understanding, theological convergences, common suffering and common prayer, shared witness and service".

In 1938, when church leaders met in Utrecht, the Netherlands, to work out the details for establishing a World Council of Churches, the word "fellowship" came immediately to mind as a way of describing the participation it would seek in a common cause. William Temple, soon to become the wartime archbishop of Canterbury, said that "the very nature of the church demands that it shall make manifest to the world the unity in Christ of all who believe in him. We may not pretend that the existing unity among Christians is greater than it in fact is; but we should act upon it as far as it is already a reality."

Temple's words point to two key elements of this fellowship. First, as veteran ecumenist and missionary Lesslie Newbigin – who spent much of his life as a bishop of the united Church of South India – has said, this is a reality richer than is often suggested by the English word "fellowship" – a group of individuals who decide to come together for some reason. The fellowship of churches in the WCC depends on a reality that already exists long before they decide to come together – namely their "common participation in the reality of the triune God through the incarnation and atonement wrought in Christ and through the continuing work of the Holy Spirit". What Temple called "the unity in Christ of all who believe in him" is something given, not something to be achieved by founding or joining "a fellowship of churches".

Yet also, and second, this fellowship is based on a pledge to make this given unity manifest. The WCC seeks unity that is visible; it does not rest content with a mere agreement about the mystical unity of all Christians in the triune God. In 1950, one of the first meetings of the central committee of the new WCC spoke at some length on what it means to be a "fellowship of churches", noting that member churches "recognize that the membership of the church of Christ is more inclusive than the membership of their own church body. They seek, therefore, to enter into living contact with those outside their own ranks who confess the Lordship of Christ."

• The most obvious evidence of the "living contact" is in the simple fact of being together. This – for all the limitations that remain – is an ever astonishing reality. Just how astonishing it is may not be so evident today, when cooperation among churches that would have been unthinkable two generations ago can be taken for granted. As Sweden's Archbishop Yngve Brilioth wrote at the time of the Amsterdam assembly, if the representatives of the churches gathered there had been consistent with their own histories "they should have separated with an anathema".

The numerous conferences and meetings organized by the WCC provide the clearest opportunities for Christians of different confessions, nations, races, cultures, political, social and economic backgrounds to be together. As they witness to their experiences, as they tell their stories, as they test their insights, the fellowship is strengthened. Those who take part in such encounters are again and again inspired to encourage in their own churches a sense of solidarity with Christians in distant parts of the world, a greater sensitivity to the needs of their own setting and a new commitment to the breaking down of the inherited barriers between churches at the local level. For more than fifty years now, the WCC has led in the setting up of many signs, smaller or greater, of the realization of Christ's prayer that the unity of his followers might be visible "so that the world may believe" (John 17:21).

• But this togetherness in the fellowship of the WCC is not just an inspiring symbol. In their message to the churches, the delegates to the first assembly said: God "has

The WCC's first assembly in Amsterdam, Netherlands (1948). From left to right: W.A. Visser 't Hooft, Geoffrey Fisher, John Mott, and Archbishop Germanos Photo Oikoumene

brought us here together in Amsterdam... Christ has made us His own, and He is not divided. In seeking Him we find one another. Here at Amsterdam we have committed ourselves afresh to Him, and have convenanted with one another in constituting this World Council of Churches. We intend to stay together." In so doing, they pointed to a commitment to fellowship that would transcend polite encounters and warm feelings, and would face up to the reasons for their divisions. Naturally, this has made for tensions, sometimes severe, within the fellowship of the Council, though few churches have broken away. Nor is progress always evident in dealing with the deepest of these divergences. Yet while its highest ideals remain to be fully achieved, the WCC has been marked by the prevalence of the will to stay together over the inclination to excommunicate those with whom one disagrees.

• The Basis makes clear that this fellowship into which the member churches have entered has implications. The WCC is not "its own reason for being". Rather, the churches in the fellowship of the Council "seek to fulfil together their common calling". Being together and staying together lead inevitably to working together. The churches, in the words of the Council's first general secretary, W.A. Visser 't Hooft, "come together as pilgrims with the same goal and the same marching orders".

In later chapters we shall look more closely at the specific ways the churches have been working out this common calling. Here we pick out three elements.

First, the words "common calling" imply a *vocation,* a sense of being called by God. This is beyond mere activism; it is no less a clear rejection of passively accepting the way things are in either the church or the world. "Let us find out those things in each place which we can do together now, and faithfully do them," said the WCC's third assembly in New Delhi (1961), "praying and working always for that fuller unity which Christ wills for his church." The central committee in 1972, noting how efforts to fulfil the common calling may lead to tensions, said, "We can witness to our experience that there is in Christ that which binds us together despite ourselves. In witnessing, we can but press on to make full use of that fellowship for greater justice."

Second, this common calling is something *dynamic.* The "marching orders" are never static. The things which the churches are called to do together will differ from one time to another, and from one place to another, for the world into which the church is called, indeed *sent* on mission, is constantly changing.

The fact that the churches' common calling implies change and renewal suggests another dimension of the fellowship: *growing together.* This is often challenging, sometimes even painful, for it implies a willingness to take the risk of changing, increasingly coming to see one's own church as an expression of a worldwide and united community of Christians rather than focusing only on its limited particularities.

Third, the final words of the Basis point to a further dimension: the churches are to fulfil their common calling "to the glory of the one God, Father, Son and Holy Spirit". These trinitarian words at the end of the Basis are not just a liturgical refrain or a theological affirmation about the nature of God. They suggest, as has been the case, that *worshipping together* is central to every meeting of the World Council of Churches.

These periods of corporate prayer and Bible study, enriched by songs and intercessions and the witness from Christian traditions in many cultures, point beyond themselves to the rootedness of the churches' fellowship in the very being of God. To be sure, worshipping together in the fellowship of the WCC offers only an imperfect foreshadowing of the "great and promised feast", since it is not yet able to extend to a eucharistic celebration of all Christians around the same table.

Yet common worship visibly affirms the source of the hope in which the churches undertake their common tasks. It provides occasion not only to confess the shortcomings of the churches' commitment to their common calling but also to be assured of divine forgiveness and support. It witnesses to the links of those worshipping not only with fellow believers elsewhere in the world but also with Christians of preceding ages. It expresses gratitude for evidence of God's blessing of the churches' common undertakings while pleading for continued divine guidance and grace. And it offers a public testimony to the glory and love of God.

A statement from the WCC's seventh assembly captured the hope and commitment implied in this trinitarian faith. "In spite of all the dangers and difficulties of the world, we are moved not to despair, but to joy in the promises of the triune God. Created by God, saved by Christ, we rejoice in the power of the Holy Spirit, the Spirit of freedom and truth, the Spirit at work in history, the Spirit which continually opens the future before us. Come, Holy Spirit, have mercy on us; renew and empower us to be your witnesses to the world!"

* * *

Prior to the eighth assembly, the member churches of the WCC were invited to participate in a process of reflection and study on a "Common Understanding and Vision of the WCC". The insights and perspectives generated in the course of this process found expression in a policy statement entitled "Towards a Common Understanding and Vision of the World Council of Churches" which the central committee adopted in 1997. The central chapter of this document on "The Self-Understanding of the World Council of Churches" represents in fact a renewed and updated interpretation of the Basis and in particular its characterization of the Council as a "fellowship of churches" and its emphasis on the "common calling" which the churches seek to fulfil in and through the Council. On the first point, the document says: "The essence of the Council is the relationship of the churches to one another. The Council *is* the fellowship of churches on the way towards full *koinonia*. It *has* a structure and organization in order to serve as an instrument for the churches as they work towards *koinonia* in faith, life and witness; but the WCC is not to be identified with this structure, nor can it serve the churches effectively apart from the constant renewal of their own ecumenical vision and commitment."

Having unfolded some of the implications of defining the WCC as "a fellowship of churches", we turn next to look at how the consciousness of this fellowship and the desire to deepen and enlarge it have taken organizational form in the World Council of Churches.

2. The Ecumenical Movement

Has the church of Christ ever truly fulfilled its calling?

Had the church continued to resemble the portrait of the earliest Christian community given in the Acts of the Apostles 2:44-47, the World Council of Churches would not have become necessary.

In these verses, summing up the situation just after Pentecost, the biblical historian describes a fellowship that seems truly to correspond to what Jesus had in mind when he prayed for his followers "that they may all be one... so that the world may believe" (John 17:21). The community of the earliest Christians in Jerusalem shared its material resources and celebrated regular and joyful worship, making its unity visible to all around and attracting more and more people to join it:

> All who believed were together and had all things in common; they would sell their possessions and goods and distribute the proceeds to all, as any had need. Day by day, as they spent much time together in the temple, they broke bread at home and they ate their food with glad and generous hearts, praising God and having the goodwill of all the people. And day by day the Lord added to their number those who were being saved.

But the next chapters of Acts record a series of events that strained this unity almost from the beginning. Forces that would divide the church in later centuries are foreshadowed here – greed, lack of commitment, racial exclusiveness, lust for power, theological differences, personality conflicts, opposition from outside.

Acts 5 tells the story of Ananias and Sapphira. Perhaps from selfishness, perhaps wanting to ensure their security in case things did not work out, they were not prepared for total commitment. They held back some of the proceeds when they sold their land – which was their right – but tried to give the impression of having wholeheartedly joined the community. Acts 6 introduces the unhappy spectre of ethnic conflict, as "the Hellenists murmured against the Hebrews because their widows were neglected in the daily distribution".

Internal difficulties were not the only problem. Many of Jerusalem's religious leaders did not look kindly on the growing fellowship, and their opposition reached new heights after Stephen's martyrdom (Acts 7-8). Persecution scattered the Christians. Among those who came into contact with them outside of Jerusalem was a magician named Simon, who saw the gift of the Holy Spirit as a way to enhance his personal popularity as an entertainer and even offered to pay the apostles for access to this power (Acts 8:9-21).

The spread of the gospel to Gentiles soon raised the question of whether Jewish ceremonial regulations should apply to them (Acts 10-11). This earliest of what would be many theological clashes over the centuries nearly split the apostles themselves. Eventually it required a council (Acts 15:1-29) to resolve the difficulties.

At the same time, personality conflicts appeared among the leaders of the young church. One, recorded in Acts 15, pitted Paul against Barnabas. A "sharp disagreement" which arose between the two over whether to take John Mark along on a missionary journey ended with the two going their separate ways.

Other passages of the New Testament and writings of later church historians continue the dismaying story of divisions within the body for whose unity Christ had prayed. With the conversion of Constantine in the 4th century, the church achieved official status in the Roman empire. But one consequence of replacing persecution with power was that secular political issues and rivalries came, directly or indirectly, onto the church's agenda.

Charges and counter-charges of false teaching, as well as disputes over power and influence, plagued the church over the centuries. From time to time, ecumenical councils – gatherings of bishops from throughout the oikoumene, the "whole inhabited earth" (as they then knew it) – were convened in order to settle these differences by establishing true Christian teaching.

Three lasting divisions

Three divisions of the church have had especially far-reaching consequences.

1. While the whole church agreed that Jesus Christ was fully God and fully human, some did not accept the formulation by the mid-5th century council of Chalcedon of how the divine and human natures are united in his person. (Thus the determination of which councils merit the name "ecumenical" is itself a subject of interchurch disagreement.) As often happens, a complex doctrinal dispute was aggravated by cultural, political, economic and personal factors; and some scholars see the eventual break more as a revolt by churches outside the empire against Graeco-Roman domination than as a theological split.

The so-called "non-Chalcedonian" churches of Egypt (Coptic), Syria, Ethiopia, Armenia and India are known as the Oriental Orthodox family. In 1990, after more than 25 years of discussion stimulated by their fellowship within the WCC, a commission of Oriental and Eastern Orthodox church leaders and theologians agreed that the differences which led to their 1500-year-old estrangement were a case of expressing the same truth through different formulas, and that churches from the two families should now move towards restoring full communion.

2. In the centuries after the council of Chalcedon, conflict raged about the respective authority of the bishops of Rome and Constantinople, climaxing in the mid-11th century division between the Eastern and Western churches. The former are the Eastern Orthodox churches; heirs of the latter are the Roman Catholic Church and those churches which later broke away from it. The sixteen Eastern Orthodox churches are self-governing in their domestic affairs. Most of them are autocephalous, i.e. entirely self-governing, and members of the WCC. The Ecumenical Patriarch of Constantinople is "first among equals" of the Orthodox primates. The Roman Catholic Church, which is not a WCC member, retains the idea of the universal primacy and jurisdiction of the bishop of Rome.

3. Several movements of dissent arose within the Western church from time to time, but the most convulsive was the series of breaks with Rome in the 16th century, grouped

under the name of the Protestant Reformation. Zealous for renewal, the Reformation churches also proved to be prone to divisiveness. Although the major Reformers all professed a commitment to Christian unity, disputes about theology, as well as political, social, ethnic and economic strife, drove Protestant Christians apart.

First stirrings towards a new unity

Yet amidst all the divisions in the church, there were always a few who kept alive the ideal of unity. The credit for first suggesting regular meetings of people from the many separate churches, so that they could listen to one another, understand each other's points of view, and plan how best to work alongside and with, rather than against, one another goes to the English Baptist missionary William Carey. In 1806, from his base across the river from Calcutta, he wrote to his supporters in London to propose that they arrange for a "general association of all denominations of Christians, from the four quarters of the world, kept about once in ten years', to meet for the first time at the Cape of Good Hope.

Still more significant, however, was what grew out of the "immediate response" in 1722 of the 22-year old Count Nicolaus von Zinzendorf, of Dresden, Germany, when asked by a refugee carpenter to give land on the estate he had inherited a year before to a persecuted group from Moravia. The community of these Moravians, who knew themselves as "the Hidden Seed", was a remnant of the followers of Jan Hus persecuted by the Counter-Reformation in the Czech lands.

Within ten years the humble community sent two of its members to live and witness among the slaves in the Caribbean island of St Thomas, and by ten years later 68 missionaries had begun serving in over twenty countries in six continents. They went with an expectation of serving alongside every type of existing church, and established solidarity with the poorest and most downtrodden people wherever they went. Their influence extended to many of the subsequent Protestant missionary movements and leaders, including John Wesley and the young William Carey.

And so, throughout the 19th century, at first in Europe and then in North America, persons, groups, Christian organizations and eventually whole churches began to understand that the message of Jesus deserved to be responded to by a single, united fellowship, not by a plethora of competing denominations.

Lay movements show the way

The first ecumenical organization with this vision was the Young Men's Christian Association, founded in 1844 and growing out of the prayer and Bible study meetings of young men serving in grocers' shops in London around the young George Williams. Their first world congress was in Paris in 1855, which made the phrase "Jesus Christ as God and Saviour according to the holy scriptures" central to their Basis. The Young Women's Christian Association followed soon after, in 1855 in England and in 1894 at the world level. A third lay movement, following the same path of independent gatherings of committed young Christians, produced – at national level – the Student Christian Movements and the Student Volunteer Missionary Unions and – at international level – the World Student Christian Federation.

Officially these Christian youth and student movements were not attached to any specific churches and so had no part in the founding of the WCC. Yet many would say that they played the most significant roles in the rise of the movements both for world mission and for Christian unity.

Alongside these, still key actors in the ecumenical movement in many parts of the world, the 19th and 20th centuries have seen the rise – and sometimes the fall – of a host of other ecumenical organizations and agencies: for common prayer, for foreign missions, for friendship across national frontiers, for publishing materials from different churches, for service to elderly people and many other groups, for peace, for the study of the Bible or specific areas of theological concern, for social concern and action, and so on. Virtually all of these exist first and foremost at the local level, giving rise to national offices and leaders, sometimes also to groupings at international level. And as the ecumenical movement comes to be accepted (see below) by whole churches, so again local groupings of congregations and specific groups within them spring into life, as do shared, inter-church, agencies and partnerships at national and international levels.

In the early stages many of these were non-denominational, i.e. they did not take account of which church their members were also members of, and would on the whole either presuppose that everyone agreed on central points or else rule out any discussion of contentious items. But the YMCA and its sister lay movements soon realized that their members should not be expected to forget about their particular church loyalties; the movement hoped rather to encourage young people in and for their church, and gradually came to realize that positive and carefully prepared discussion of the points of difference between the churches could not only become an instrument for the growth of their members but also point to ways the divided churches could come to appreciate each other's experience, and so grow into unity. The key lay movements knew themselves called to be interdenominational.

The churches become involved

In mission. The world missionary conference in Edinburgh, Scotland, in 1910 is often called the birthplace of the modern ecumenical movement. As we have seen, it was from among the missionaries, serving peoples other than those they were born into, that the call for a "whole church taking the whole gospel into the whole world" was first heard.

For as they crossed land and sea to preach the good news among other peoples and cultures, many of them came to see that the differences of doctrine, church government and style of worship, which so sorely divided their churches at home, are rooted in historical controversies with little relevance in the countries to which God had sent them. Moreover, pro-

The global mission conference at Edinburgh, Scotland, in 1910 is often called the "birth-place of the ecumenical movement" Photo Oikoumene

claiming the good news in all the world was clearly a far greater task than any single mission society could fulfil by itself. Under such circumstances, any inability to work together was recognized as a scandal.

Joint planning, cooperative mission schemes and agreements that assigned different regions to different denominations did not entirely do away with rivalry among the sending churches. So the demand for greater unity in mission persisted and grew. William Carey's proposal for a first meeting in 1810 met with little more than scepticism from his supporters, but several international gatherings of Protestants from different churches involved in mission were held in the second half of the 19th century.

Edinburgh was originally planned as the third in one of those series. But it was different from the earlier in two key respects. First, those participating were official delegates of the mission organizations of particular churches. That made it a gathering which could speak both to and for the divided churches. Second, it was restricted to missionary organizations working among "non-Christian peoples", thus excluding for example denominations and societies operating in Europe, the Middle East or Latin America. The consequence of not inviting those who were seeking to persuade people to leave one church for another, says church historian Kenneth Scott Latourette, was to make possible a greater inclusiveness of theological convictions in the ecumenical movement.

Participants from what were then called "younger churches" were few at Edinburgh – seventeen out of 1200. But their visibility was high, and their contribution marked the beginning of what Latourette called a welcome "trend to embrace older and younger churches on terms of equality".

A continuation committee appointed at Edinburgh served as a key instrument of missionary cooperation across national and denominational boundaries, until in 1921 it could be re-formed into the International Missionary Council. This Council, before becoming fully integrated into the World Council of Churches in 1961, sponsored a series of missionary conferences (Jerusalem 1928; Tambaram, South India 1938; Whitby, Canada 1947; Willingen, Germany 1952; and Ghana 1958, where the decision to seek integration into the WCC was finally taken) and meanwhile built many structures for cooperation and common planning at national and regional levels.

In Faith and Order. In order to focus attention on the planting of "one undivided church of Christ in each non-Christian nation", the planners of the Edinburgh conference had deliberately kept discussion of doctrinal and church order differences off the agenda.

But one of the delegates, US Episcopalian Charles Brent, at the time a missionary bishop in the Philippines, became convinced that "whenever God gives a vision he also points to a new responsibility". At an early-morning Anglican eucharist he received a vision of the task of a comparable conference devoted to precisely those questions of faith and of order that would need to be resolved before a truly united church could arise. So at his own church's convention later in 1910 he persuaded it to invite "all Christian communions throughout the world which confess our Lord Jesus Christ as God and Saviour" to a global conference on these other themes.

After years of correspondence, personal contacts and preparatory meetings, some 400 people, most of them official delegates from over 100 churches, came together in Lausanne, Switzerland, in August 1927 for the first world conference on Faith and Order.

The seven sections of the Lausanne agenda took up topics with which theological discussion still wrestles: (1) Christian unity, (2) the church's message, (3) the nature of the church, (4) a common confession of faith, (5) ordained ministry, (6) the sacraments, and (7) the unity of Christendom and the place of the different churches in it. The breadth of the theological gulf between Christian confessions is disclosed by the report of a brief exchange in section 4: after an Eastern Orthodox delegate insisted that "we must declare our loyalty to the Nicene Creed", a Congregationalist stood up to say, "Well, I think we should clear all that old lumber out of the way"!

In Life and Work. The most controversial report at Lausanne was that of section 7 which called for the churches to collaborate in "applied Christianity", specifically through the World Alliance for Promoting International Friendship through the Churches, and the Life and Work movement. Both these bodies had grown out of international Christian peace movements, the urgency of whose message had been heightened by the horrors of the first world war. Church leaders from neutral countries, especially Sweden's Archbishop Nathan Söderblom, had sought unsuccessfully to prevent the war; and when the fighting stopped Söderblom was active in organizing the universal Christian conference on Life and Work, which met in Stockholm in 1925.

Some delegates in Lausanne had feared that collaboration on "applied Christianity" would give interchurch cooperation on social issues precedence over the search for church unity. This tension was to resurface again and again in different forms over the years ahead.

In fact, the distinction between "Faith and Order" and "Life and Work" was already then not so neat. The conviction of the early Life and Work movement that "doctrine divides and service unites" soon gave way to a recognition that decisions about what kind of social action can best be undertaken in common have much to do with such theological issues as the meaning of the "kingdom of God".

Growing awareness of this inseparability, a sense that the number of ecumenical initiatives springing up was confusing and counter-productive, and a recognition that, if efforts for church unity were to take hold, the churches had to be officially involved, led to decisions taken by both Faith and Order and Life and Work at their 1937 world conferences in Edinburgh and Oxford to form a joint committee to plan for their merger in a world council of churches.

At its meeting in Utrecht, the Netherlands, the next year, this committee resolved most of the vital questions about how such a council should be organized. Willem A. Visser 't Hooft, at the time general secretary of the WSCF, was invited to hold the comparable office in the new council, in partnership with the IMC's William Paton and Henry Smith Leiper – a post Visser 't Hooft was to hold until his retirement in 1966. A provisional committee was appointed and an inaugural assembly planned for August 1941, though it was delayed because of the outbreak of the second world war in September 1939. It finally took place in 1948.

Meanwhile another important area of dawning ecumenical cooperation between the churches was Christian education. The World's Sunday School Association – founded in 1907, reorganized in 1924, and renamed the World Council of Christian Education (WCCE) in 1947 – was a federation of national and international bodies concerned with improving the quality of lesson materials and teacher training. Its roots were in the Sunday school movement begun in 1780 by Robert Raikes in England. It followed the developments towards a World Council of Churches with interest, and was to be integrated into the WCC in 1971.

1948-54: Amsterdam to Evanston

"Man's Disorder and God's Design" was the theme of the WCC's first assembly. Sobered by the disorder of the post-war world, but confident that "God is himself at work rebuilding his own order", 351 delegates from 147 churches assembled in Amsterdam. On Monday 23 August 1948 they approved with no dissenting votes the resolution "that the formation of the World Council of Churches be declared to be and is hereby complete".

A new manifestation of international disorder at the time was the cold war, reflected in the assembly in an exchange between US Presbyterian John Foster Dulles, later his country's secretary of state, and Czech Reformed theologian Josef Hromádka. Dulles argued that the moral values essential to

A WCC staff member preparing boxes of Bibles in German, to be shipped to prisoners of war in France and England and to churches in Germany (1940s)   Photo Oikoumene

world peace were embodied, if imperfectly, by Western democracies, and that communism was the greatest threat to them. Hromádka pleaded for understanding communism as a force representing a vision of society which the Christian church and Western civilization had largely lost. The assembly did not allow this sharp difference to destroy the fellowship. Its call for a "responsible society" insisted that no civilization can escape the radical judgment of the word of God, and rejected the assumption that capitalism and communism were the only two choices available.

Agreeing that they could not know the destination of the common road on which they were setting out, delegates acknowledged that the Lord of the church "was powerfully at work... to lead us further to goals we but dimly discern". In what became Amsterdam's most quoted phrase, they summarized how they understood what the assembly had meant: "We have committed ourselves afresh to Christ and have covenanted with one another in constituting this World Council of Churches. *We intend to stay together.*"

That intention was rooted in far more than the contacts made during the assembly's two weeks. For ten years the WCC had been "in process of formation". Despite war-time limits on communication and transport (the provisional committee could not meet between 1939 and 1946), its Geneva office had coordinated a great deal of activity. By 1948 142 people were employed by the Council.

Fragile links between Christians in various countries of war-torn Europe had been maintained. By the time of the first assembly, WCC programmes of interchurch aid, service to refugees, international affairs, the Ecumenical Church Loan Fund, the Ecumenical Institute and the youth department already had several years of experience behind them. This made it possible for the WCC to get off to a running start.

Post-war reconstruction was seen as an *ecumenical* task, aimed at rebuilding "the whole life of the fellowship of churches which finds expression in the WCC". One challenge was presented by the 12 million people who had been displaced by the war. Although caring for them and integrating them into local communities was understood as a task for national and regional councils of churches, aid to refugees called for specialized legal knowledge and familiarity with the resources of the numerous international, governmental and voluntary agencies. Because few churches had such expertise, the WCC set up a centralized service to carry out projects for refugees unable to find a country of resettlement. As soon as it was feasible these projects were turned over to local/national churches or ecumenical agencies.

The WCC thus had sizeable relief operations to report at Amsterdam, and the assembly recognized that interchurch aid could no longer be considered a temporary programme. The decision was taken to extend this concern for Christian service beyond Europe to other parts of the world, in the first instance to the Middle East, where more than 600,000 Arabs had fled from Palestine in the war that accompanied partition.

A quite different problem was posed by the need to find an appropriate way by which to give the German churches some place in the new Council. As early as October 1945 a WCC delegation travelled to Stuttgart to meet the new council of the Evangelical Church of Germany. Any uncertainty about the approach of the Germans was quickly dispelled when the German colleagues presented a "Stuttgart Declaration" in which they, on behalf of their whole church, expressed awareness that they were implicated in the guilt of the German people, their determination to make a new beginning in the life of their church, and a desire to participate fully in the new ecumenical fellowship.

The Commission of the Churches on International Affairs, set up in 1946 by the WCC and the International Missionary Council, played an important role in drafting the article on religious freedom in the Universal Declaration of Human Rights, adopted by the United Nations in December 1948.

The Korean war strained the WCC's effort to forge an ecumenical consensus across the cold-war divide. Just after the war broke out in June 1950, a central committee statement noted that "we must seek peace by expanding justice and by attempting to reconcile contending world powers", but praised the United Nations as an instrument of world order for having authorized "police action" in Korea – the only time the WCC has approved the use of military force in a particular situation. Some WCC member churches saw this statement as a political identification with the West which endangered fellowship with churches in the socialist countries.

Prior to Amsterdam, the WCC sent a questionnaire to churches around the world, asking about the role of women in their life and ministry. Among those responding were German women who told of losing positions as pastors of large congregations to which they had been assigned during the war, when men were in the army. Christian women in newly independent India spoke of their perplexity when their government urged them to get an education and take a role in society while their churches talked only of the roles of wife and mother. Women from the USA described the large women's groups in their churches, which often collected most of the money to finance church programmes but seldom had a voice in decision-making about them. The responses led to the publication of a volume *The Service and Status of Women in the Churches* by Kathleen Bliss, which was to exercise much influence in the ensuing discussions.

1954-61: Evanston to New Delhi

Among the issues that emerged at the second assembly, held in Evanston, outside Chicago, in 1954, two were to prove especially important for the WCC in the years ahead – racism and colonialism.

Segregation based on race, colour or ethnic origin is "contrary to the gospel and incompatible with the Christian doctrine of man and with the nature of the church of Christ", Evanston declared. And it urged churches to abolish racial discrimination "within their own life and within society". That provoked a reaction from the delegates of one of eight WCC member churches in South Africa, the Dutch

Reformed Church (DRC), which complained that the assembly had not taken their situation seriously. The resolution was revised to acknowledge the difficulties some churches would have in eliminating segregation at once.

The WCC had little more to say about South Africa in the next five years. But after the killing of 67 blacks by South African police at Sharpeville in March 1960 led to the declaration of a state of emergency, the WCC invited black and white church leaders in the country to meet with an international ecumenical delegation at Cottesloe College in the University of Witwatersrand. The report of the consultation – approved by 80 percent of the participants – affirmed that no Christian could be excluded from any church on grounds of race or colour, and called attention to the injustices of apartheid.

The WCC delegation hoped that the overwhelming majority by which the statement was accepted signalled a genuine breakthrough, even if it would hardly have been seen as radical anywhere else in the world. That optimism did not reckon with the strength of resistance to change in white South Africa. The prime minister publicly dismissed what Cottesloe said, and shortly thereafter the three Dutch Reformed WCC member churches withdrew from the Council.

Decolonization and "nation-building" increasingly concerned the ecumenical movement during the 1950s. The WCC had been slow to grasp the urgency of the problems facing Africa, Asia, Latin America and the Middle East. While many European and North American churches stressed that colonized peoples must be carefully prepared for independence and self-government, Christians from "younger churches" were growing more and more impatient at the slow pace of decolonization.

Already in 1952, Asian churches at a conference in Lucknow, India, insisted that the best way to meet the challenge of communism was by a positive attitude towards the social revolution taking place in East Asia. Acknowledging that communism had "awakened and challenged our conscience to see the need for action", the Lucknow conference called for radical land reform, planned economic development and church backing of struggles for self-determination. In 1955 the WCC took up this challenge and launched a programme of support for churches facing "rapid social change".

There were several points of tension. The accelerating breakdown of old social structures challenged the traditional preference for gradual reform. Despite growing secularization, most Western Christians still assumed that Christian values permeated their society and its institutions. Christian thinkers in the new nations could not share this confidence in traditional political and economic structures. They emphasized the need for a pluralistic social ethic that would promote human values in a national perspective. Mindful of the recent past in Europe, many Western churches were critical of nationalism, whereas churches in the third world stressed that the new nation-states could instil dignity and self-respect in their peoples.

Events in October 1956 created further tensions within the WCC. The central committee met in Hungary in August that year. Some Hungarian political leaders later accused the WCC of having encouraged the attempt to overthrow the regime which resulted in Soviet military intervention. Almost simultaneously came the Suez crisis, when British and French forces joined the Israelis in an attack on Egypt. The WCC officers responded by recalling the Evanston declaration that nations should "refrain from the threat or use of force against the territorial integrity of any state". That criticism upset a number of French church leaders.

1961-68: New Delhi to Uppsala

Holding the third assembly in 1961 in New Delhi, India, symbolized the WCC's dawning, if still incomplete, recognition of what it means to be a world body. Eighteen of the 23 churches newly admitted to membership by the assembly were from Africa, Asia and Latin America. Four others were large Eastern European Orthodox churches – in Russia, Romania, Bulgaria and Poland. The vote to receive them was nearly unanimous, showing that East-West political tension was not a decisive factor for ecumenical relations.

Another important sign of growth at New Delhi was the integration of the International Missionary Council into the WCC. The two bodies had always had a close working relationship, but there had been resistance on both sides to a merger. Some groups within the IMC distrusted the WCC's theological stands; and for some Orthodox churches in the WCC, mission automatically raised fears of attempts by Western Christians to lure away their members.

In sharp contrast to the second assembly, which the archbishop of Chicago had forbidden Catholics to attend, the Vatican sent observers to New Delhi. A few weeks after the assembly ended, Pope John XXIII announced that a Second Vatican Council would be convened in 1962. The WCC accepted an invitation to send observers to it; and in 1965 the WCC and the Vatican agreed to establish a Joint Working Group, which has since met annually to coordinate relations between the WCC and the Roman Catholic Church.

Besides enabling ecumenical response to human suffering around the world, the WCC was helping churches to rethink the idea of Christian service (diakonia). Several consultations in the early 1960s on the role of institutional Christian service fed into an international gathering at Swanwick, UK, in 1966. It said that the idea of diakonia must be extended beyond "charitable" relief and service to programmes of social advancement.

On the heels of the Swanwick meeting came the world conference on "Church and Society" in Geneva in 1966, the WCC's most serious attempt to understand the revolutionary changes taking place in culture, politics, economics and science and technology. The majority of the 420 participants invited were lay people. Yet more important, half came from outside the North Atlantic region. All the main confessional traditions were well represented, and a team of Catholic observers attended.

The Geneva conference insisted that revolutionary action, whatever support Christians might give it, could not escape

During the conference on "Church and Society" in Geneva (1966), participants marched to the United Nations "to affirm and support the vision of a just and peaceful world embodied in the ideal of the UN"
Photo Oikoumene

the judgment of biblical faith on all human action. In regard to economics, for example, the conference report focused on economic justice rather than on passing moral judgments for or against any particular economic system.

This conference enabled the WCC to mobilize the churches' resources for more effective social action by pointing to the need for new strategies and a global perspective. But voices in the church calling for militant action in favour of the poor were growing louder. These people were impatient with what they saw as the "moderate" social ethics of the ecumenical mainstream, including the Geneva conference. That impatience was amplified by the political and social climate in many parts of the world in the late 1960s. The ecumenical movement was coming under increasing pressure to commit itself more definitively to radical political action for justice and freedom.

One step taken shortly before the fourth assembly was the establishment of a joint agency by the WCC and the Roman Catholic Church, charged with furthering cooperation in the fields of society, development and peace, and consequently called SODEPAX. This agency published a series of reports at the turn of the 1970s, one of which, on the theology of development, included a long article by Gustavo Gutiérrez of Peru foreshadowing his famous book *The Theology of Liber-*

ation. But the independent thinking and the dynamism for which SODEPAX quickly became known made difficulties for the two sponsoring bodies, and it was first severely cut and then phased out in the late 1970s.

1968-75: Uppsala to Nairobi

More than any other WCC assembly, Uppsala 1968 is associated with radical change in the Council. The atmosphere was highly charged, reflecting alike the tense world situation in that turbulent year and the ferment among students and other young people which had bubbled over in Paris, Tokyo, Berkeley (California) and many other cities. The assembly could not escape this pressure. Sit-ins, walk-outs, pickets and vigils made the youth presence highly visible, and often audible in its critique of the Council.

Economic and social justice remained high on the agenda, with special emphasis on the need to control population growth and improve food production and distribution. Recalling the Amsterdam theme, Indian economist Samuel Parmar warned that "development is *disorder*. It is revolution. Our task is to imbue the revolutionary movements of our time with creativity and to divest them of their anarchic content."

Development, said a 1970 WCC consultation, should aim at three inter-related objectives: justice, self-reliance and economic growth. The churches' task is to participate with the poor and oppressed in their struggles for that kind of development. Because existing WCC structures were seen as inadequate to give such support, the Commission on the Churches' Participation in Development (CCPD) was created. Through it, the WCC engaged in research, education, documentation and publication, and provided technical advice and financial support where possible, while enabling ecumenical exchanges among a network of local groups in many countries.

Awareness of the threat posed by racism to peace and justice remained keen. The opening sermon at the fourth assembly was to have been preached by Martin Luther King Jr, but he had been assassinated four months earlier. US black novelist James Baldwin reminded delegates of the long history of church involvement in racial injustice, and asked pointedly whether they had "the moral energy, the spiritual daring, to atone, to repent, to be born again".

Although church and ecumenical statements had consistently condemned racism, there was a strong sense of the need to go beyond exhortation to action. So in 1969 the WCC set up its Programme to Combat Racism (PCR). Its emphasis was on combating white racism, entrenched in social, economic and political power structures, with the understanding that the victims of racism must undertake their own liberation, with outsiders playing a supportive role.

Awareness of other world religious communities and traditions was a new feature in the fourth assembly. A consultation at Kandy in Sri Lanka in March 1967 had reviewed the increasing number of efforts among Christians to envisage an appropriate policy of "dialogue". Its report was well received by the central committee of the WCC that year, and the Division of World Mission and Evangelism proceeded to pursue this new policy, knowing that by no means all the churches were sympathetic to it.

So there were tensions as well as excitement in the ecumenical fellowship over the new developments in the WCC after Uppsala. Programmes sometimes overlapped and were not easy to coordinate. Awareness of and support for what the Council was doing varied greatly among member churches. And financial difficulties imposed stringent limits on creative innovation.

Yet there was also in the Uppsala assembly a new confidence in the central purpose of the Council to "anticipate [God's] kingdom in joyful worship and daring acts", as the message put it. Recalling that the New Delhi assembly had looked to the unity "of all Christians in each place", Uppsala pointed to "a fresh understanding of the unity of all Christians in each place", and saw the WCC as "a transitional opportunity for eventually actualizing a truly universal, ecumenical, conciliar form of common life and witness".

A symbol of the growing relationship between the WCC and the Roman Catholic Church was Pope Paul VI's visit in 1969 to the recently opened Ecumenical Centre, the building in Geneva that houses the WCC and other interchurch agencies. It was the first such visit by a pope to an ecumenical institution. Discussion of Roman Catholic membership in the WCC, which had been broached in Uppsala, most notably by the chief Vatican observer Fr Roberto Tucci, was however to be quietly shelved in 1972, even though the report published that year by the Joint Working Group had concluded that there are no insuperable theological or canonical objections to it. Roman Catholic involvement in the ecumenical movement at all levels nonetheless increased in the 1970s, with several bishops' conferences joining national councils of churches. Nearly all WCC programme units established contacts with their counterparts in the Roman Catholic Church.

1975-83: Nairobi to Vancouver

The WCC's fifth assembly in Nairobi, Kenya, in late 1975 was the first in Africa, though the site was a last-minute choice after plans to hold it in Indonesia had to be dropped.

Participants of other faiths at the presentation of the first sub-theme at the WCC's sixth assembly in Vancouver, "Life, a Gift of God" (1983)

Few African countries had been independent when the WCC was founded, but by the mid-1970s some African church leaders were arguing that the massive flow of outside funds and personnel into their churches had replaced the burdens of the colonial past with new forms of domination and dependency. Calls for a "moratorium" on sending people and money, to enable these churches to develop their own identity, had been discussed at the WCC's world mission conference in Bangkok in 1972. Nairobi voted to continue that debate by inaugurating a decade-long study of the "ecumenical sharing of resources".

Nairobi was the first assembly to which persons of other faiths – a Buddhist, a Hindu, a Jew, a Muslim and a Sikh – were officially invited as guests. During heated discussions about interfaith relations, many delegates expressed fears that dialogue with people of other faiths would inevitably weaken concern for mission and lead to syncretism.

This debate was the background to a consultation in 1977 in Chiang Mai, Thailand, on the purpose and practice of such dialogue. It drafted "Guidelines for Dialogue" which the central committee subsequently accepted. These became the basis not only of work undertaken by the WCC Dialogue sub-unit, but also of a growing number of interfaith programmes in churches around the world.

Human rights also proved a thorny topic at the Nairobi assembly. The most protracted debate arose over a long letter from two Russian churchmen, asking for action in support of what they called "confessors of faith" within the USSR. After a sometimes bitter discussion, the general secretary was asked to ensure that religious liberty would become the subject of consultations with member churches in the countries that had signed the 1975 Helsinki Agreement.

More than a fifth of the delegates to Nairobi were women. If that percentage was far from reflecting women's role in church life, it was a great improvement over earlier assemblies. Nairobi called for a major WCC study of the "Community of Women and Men in the Church". Starting with the experiences of women in churches and societies in different areas, this study involved more than 150 local groups, whose materials provided background for its concluding international conference in Sheffield, UK, in 1981.

The search for "a just, participatory and sustainable society" provided the framework for much of the Council's activities in these years. One central theme was the impact of science and technology on this search. Three years of preparatory work by theologians and scientists went into a world conference on "Faith, Science and the Future", in July 1979, which drew more than 400 official participants and 500 visitors to the Massachusetts Institute of Technology, outside Boston, USA.

This conference made it clear that the prolonged faith-science debate had moved into a new stage. Participants from the third world said industrially advanced societies were using science and technology to serve their own military and economic interests in ways that brought about great suffering in "our part of the world".

Many of the scientists present, some of whom had worked on developing nuclear weapons, pleaded for a halt to the nuclear arms race, resulting in a proposal for an international public hearing on nuclear disarmament. This took place in Amsterdam in November 1981. Seventeen church leaders heard testimony from 40 "witnesses" from a wide spectrum of theological, technical, political and military perspectives. The findings, published under the title *Before It's Too Late*, concluded that the time had come for the churches to declare it a crime against humanity not only to use but even to produce nuclear weapons.

The fifth assembly observed that, although the means and resources exist to eradicate poverty around the globe, the number of poor people is steadily increasing. CCPD's programme on "The Church and the Poor" confronted member churches with this challenge; and the 1980 world mission conference in Melbourne, Australia, described the poor as a key criterion for mission work today. Strong new initiatives coming from the churches of the oppressed were indicating "a change in the direction of mission".

This fed into the continuing debates about the purposes and priorities of mission and evangelism. After extensive consultations, the WCC central committee received a document entitled "Mission and Evangelism: An Ecumenical Affirmation" and referred it to the churches for study. It remains a key text, if deliberately brief, for both study and practice.

At its 1982 meeting in Lima, Peru, the WCC Faith and Order commission agreed that its many years of effort to put into words the growing ecumenical convergence about baptism, eucharist and ministry had reached the point where the text should be submitted to the churches for official response. These three church-dividing issues had been on the commission's agenda as far back as the first Faith and Order world conference in 1927. The resulting Lima text has been distributed in hundreds of thousands of copies in dozens of languages, and is surely the most discussed text ever produced by the WCC (see pp. 150-57).

The Faith and Order plenary commission meeting in Lima, Peru (1982)
WCC

Yet the WCC action in these years that aroused the most attention in the world's media, thanks to the wave of protest in the USA and elsewhere that greeted it, was the grant in 1978 of US$85,000 from the Special Fund of the Programme to Combat Racism for the humanitarian work of the Patriotic Front of Zimbabwe-Rhodesia, then engaged in an armed struggle to overthrow the white minority regime of Ian Smith.

PCR's Special Fund had made annual grants for several years to organizations of the racially oppressed and to groups supporting victims of racism – for humanitarian activities such as education, legal defence and refugee work. This Fund symbolized the churches' solidarity against racial oppression; the grant to the Patriotic Front showed just how clearly a symbol can speak. It came to be a focal point for attacks on the WCC as a whole, from the white communities in Southern Africa and their backers in the West. In the ensuing controversy the WCC's role in supporting negotiations for the independence of Zimbabwe over many years tended to be overlooked.

1983-91: Vancouver to Canberra

The WCC's sixth assembly, in Vancouver, Canada, in 1983, has been called "a glorious patchwork" and "a worshipping assembly". Neither the diversity of participants nor the importance of worship was new to such gatherings, but at Vancouver the crowds present (as many as 4500 a day), the variety of activities taking place (often simultaneously) and the memorably fresh acts of worship in a large yellow-and-white tent that became the symbol of the assembly, created especially vivid memories of an inclusive and worldwide Christian community.

One highlight of the worship in Vancouver was the celebration of the eucharist according to a liturgy reflecting the convergence in the Lima text on *Baptism, Eucharist and Ministry*. The archbishop of Canterbury presided, joined by six ministers from other traditions and parts of the world. Those who read scripture and led prayers included Roman Catholics and Orthodox Christians, whose official norms

Robert Runcie, archbishop of Canterbury, presided at the Lima liturgy at the Vancouver assembly (1983)

generally preclude them from receiving communion in services under the auspices of other churches.

The assembly theme was "Jesus Christ – the Life of the World". In affirming life in response to the threats posed by forces of death, Vancouver insisted that the struggle for justice and the struggle for peace may not be separated, and that engagement in this single struggle is a matter of the church's faith. Its statement on peace and justice called on the churches to condemn unequivocally, on ethical and theological grounds, the production and deployment as well as the use of nuclear weapons as a crime against humanity.

The 1980s saw growing ecumenical questioning of the styles and structures of the churches' massive operations for meeting human needs. Earlier optimism about development as a way of moving beyond charity had given way to a sense of frustration that the churches – and the people – are losing the battle for justice.

Two major international meetings addressed this concern from different angles. Three hundred persons came to Larnaca,

Cyprus, in November 1986 for a WCC consultation on interchurch aid. Insisting that the poor and oppressed people at the margins of the world's concern should be the centre of Christian service, Larnaca described diakonia as "liberating and transforming, suffering and empowering". Christian service cannot be separated from the struggle for justice and peace.

A year later, 250 persons came to El Escorial, Spain, for a consultation that climaxed the WCC's ten-year discussion of the ecumenical sharing of resources. A central emphasis was the need to recognize not only money and material goods but also churches' spiritual, theological and cultural gifts – and, perhaps most important, their testimonies of suffering – as resources to be shared. The commitments made by the participants at El Escorial highlighted identifying with the oppressed, accepting marginalized people as equal partners in decision-making, challenging the root causes and structures of injustice, and overcoming divisions between evangelism and action in society.

The huge yellow and white tent set up for the Vancouver assembly became the symbol of a new style of worship at WCC meetings   WCC

Such issues were set in a wider framework by what came to be Vancouver's best-known emphasis – the call to "a conciliar process of mutual commitment for justice, peace and the integrity of creation" (JPIC). Addressed by the assembly to WCC member churches, the scope of this appeal for a common struggle against injustice, war and environmental degradation was broadened to other churches (including the Roman Catholic Church), ecumenical organizations, action groups and people of other faiths. Built up from local, national and regional engagements, the JPIC process emphasized how the threats to life in the areas of justice, peace and the integrity of creation are interconnected.

As shown earlier, justice and peace have been prominent ecumenical concerns since the outset of the movement. "The integrity of creation" was a new phrase, linking the Christian belief in God as Creator with growing fears about threats to the habitability of the earth. An international consultation in 1988 sought to clarify the phrase and delineate some of its implications for the churches and the WCC.

The process launched in Vancouver climaxed in a world convocation in Seoul, Korea, in 1990. Participants approved an "Act of Covenanting": to work together (1) for a just economic order; (2) for the demilitarization of international relations; (3) for preserving the earth's atmosphere from global warming; and (4) for the eradication of racism and discrimination.

A quarter century after Cottesloe, the entrenchment of racism in South Africa's apartheid system continued to preoccupy many in the WCC. Vivid demonstrations of the persistence of ecumenical opposition to apartheid and to the effects South African policies were having on its neighbours came in four WCC-organized meetings in Zimbabwe and Zambia in 1985-88.

Slowly, changes began to come. Namibia, long held by South Africa in defiance of United Nations resolutions and international public opinion, became independent. And then the release of Nelson Mandela in 1990 rekindled hopes for a democratic South Africa.

The Ecumenical Decade of the Churches in Solidarity with Women ended in a festival just before the WCC's eighth assembly in Harare (1998). This mural was created during the hearing on violence against women: "I have made a handprint, a sacred one, for I am imago Dei"
WCC/Chris Black

At Easter 1988 an Ecumenical Decade of Churches in Solidarity with Women, building on activities all round the world, was launched. The decision to organize this came when the central committee judged in 1985 that the UN-sponsored International Women's Decade (1975-85) had had little impact on the churches, and that the position of women in many churches had not improved over these years. Indeed a survey by the WCC's sub-unit on Women had concluded that churches "mirrored existing social values or even lagged behind the progress of the secular world in this domain".

1991-98: Canberra to Harare

"Come Holy Spirit – Renew the Whole Creation" was the theme of the seventh assembly in Canberra, Australia, in 1991. Delegates testified that such renewal would go beyond any manifestations of what some politicians were calling "a new world order". A long-feared and devastating war had just broken out in the Persian Gulf, and this cast a shadow over the proceedings. Hours of debate, at first in the committees, and then for a full day in plenary session, could not entirely bridge the deep differences of evaluation of that situation among the churches.

At the same time this assembly experienced a moving welcome from the Australian churches which had given prominence to their Aboriginal members as the first Australians. To reach the tent for the opening act of worship all participants had to pass through the smoke of a sacred fire, and Aboriginal speakers were prominent in the programme, as were singers and dancers and the artists who contributed to an exhibition of paintings reflecting the spirituality of aboriginal peoples, mounted in the national law-courts. Children also played a role hitherto unknown in an assembly, and even led one of the morning acts of worship.

Another shadow fell over the assembly in the outrage felt by many Orthodox participants when, by an unpredicted clash of cultures, the substantial theme address by Patriarch Parthenios of Alexandria (read for him by a Greek priest, since he had stayed in the Middle East because of the Gulf war) was immediately followed by a dazzling display of drumming and dancing by young Koreans, leading into a no less substantial address by Korean woman theologian Chung Hyun Kyung, exploring a sharply different and deliberately provocative understanding of the Holy Spirit.

The 1990s turned out to be long years of brutality and unmanageable suffering: in Somalia, in the Caucasus, in the successive wars that marked the break-up of the former Yugoslavia, and perhaps above all in Rwanda – all crises that called on the solidarity, succour and sympathies of the ecumenical community. In November 1994 a first-ever WCC consultation on "Ethnicity and Nationalism – a Challenge to the Churches" was held in Sri Lanka, another country where civil strife has proved unstoppable. At the same time, the growing awareness of the economic and political dominance of the process known as globalization was coming to alarm many in the poorer countries and in the circles aware of their struggles.

A demonstration in Washington DC, USA, against the US National ▷
Rifle Association   WCC/Rick Reinhard

Guns
Are Killing
ur Children
Our Families
r Dreams

Kill
hildren
Far
Dream

Jewish Dialogue
RIES OUT

The fourth world conference on Faith and Order, held in Santiago de Compostela in Spain in 1993, agreed that a careful look must now be given to the theological issues raised by the papacy, and supported work on ecclesiology and ethics. The 1996 world mission conference held in Salvador, Brazil, explored and – above all in its worship – lived out its theme "Called to One Hope – the Gospel in Diverse Cultures".

Team visits were paid in these years to churches in every part of the world, helping them explore the challenges of the Decade of Churches in Solidarity with Women. This Decade, ending in a joyous Festival immediately before the eighth assembly in Harare, Zimbabwe, led almost without interruption into the Decade to Overcome Violence, formally called by the central committee in 1999. Within both decades, much concern was shown for the new scourge of HIV/AIDS.

The central committee met in Johannesburg in January 1994 and experienced the joy and promise of the new South Africa, eagerly awaiting its first democratic elections later that year. The WCC arranged for teams of election monitors, as it did subsequently for Malawi and Mozambique. However, a peace monitoring programme in Angola proved unable to make much difference to that country. The choice of Harare for the eighth assembly was made precisely in order to let an assembly experience that same part of the world, though by late 1998 much of the earlier joy and promise had faded, especially in Zimbabwe itself.

The central committee devoted much thought to a new text on "Towards a Common Understanding and Vision of the World Council of Churches". The final document was approved by the 1997 central committee and then explored in many of the groupings within the Harare assembly. It provided the context for a reorganization of the WCC staff into four "clusters".

And into a new century

If the 19th century, in Latourette's phrase, had been "the great century" for the expansion of the Christian faith to virtually every people and culture on earth, and the 20th – in the

President Nelson Mandela of South Africa addressing the WCC's eighth assembly in Harare (1998)

generalization of Lesslie Newbigin – "the first century since the first in which more energy and prayer has been devoted to uniting the church than into splitting it apart", what of the ecumenical movement in the 21st? Thanks to its ever-widening scope, as it has been chronicled here over the first fifty years of the WCC, the challenges remain every bit as demanding.

50

The WCC moves into a new century, struggling with the horizons of "everything that relates to the whole task of the whole church to bring the whole gospel to the whole world". Yet the confidence of the ecumenical movement has never been in the work of human beings, but rather in the love and power of God.

> We intend to stay together and are restless to grow together in unity.
> We respond to the prayer of Jesus Christ
> that all may be one in order that the world may believe (John 17:21).
> We are sustained by the assurance
> that in God's purpose all things shall be united in Christ –
> things in heaven and things on earth (Eph. 1:10).

> We affirm that what unites us is stronger than what separates us.
> Neither failures nor uncertainties
> neither fears nor threats
> will weaken our intention to continue to walk together on the way to unity,
> welcoming those who would join us on this journey,
> widening our common vision
> discovering new ways of witnessing and acting together in faith.

(from "Our Ecumenical Vision", Harare, 1998)

3. Acting Together in Faith

In chapter 1 we saw that the WCC is in essence a "fellowship of churches", and in chapter 2 how this fellowship grew out of a long history of witness and commitment. This history has continued to evolve as the churches have sought to respond in faith to events and developments in the past, often turbulent century.

So now we move from what the WCC is and where it came from to the question of what the WCC actually does. Of course, a short introduction can only point to certain key activities in what has proved over fifty years and more to have become a vast range of activities. Records of the Council's work – conference reports and minutes, newsletters and press releases, pamphlets and books – already constitute a sizeable library.

Article 3 of the WCC's Constitution, "Purposes and functions", can provide a convenient outline of the major headings. It begins by stating: "The World Council of Churches is constituted by the churches to serve the one ecumenical movement" and continues by recalling the four bodies that preceded it, whose work it is committed to taking further – Faith and Order, Life and Work, the International Missionary Council, and the World Council of Christian Education. The second paragraph sums up the purpose in a single sentence:

> The primary purpose of the fellowship of churches in the WCC is to call one another to visible unity in one faith and in one eucharistic fellowship, expressed in worship and common life in Christ, through witness and service in the world, and to advance towards that unity in order that the world may believe.

This establishes that the work of the Council is harnessed to a single and whole vision of its task, within the one faith in the purposes of the one God and for the sake of the one world God has created. It all belongs together, even if the various parts can at times look very different.

The subsequent sub-paragraphs in article 3 then each lay out key aspects of this one task. We will look at them in turn.

A. [THE CHURCHES THROUGH THE COUNCIL WILL] PROMOTE
THE PRAYERFUL SEARCH FOR FORGIVENESS AND RECONCILI-
ATION IN A SPIRIT OF MUTUAL ACCOUNTABILITY, THE DEVEL-
OPMENT OF DEEPER RELATIONSHIPS THROUGH THEOLOGICAL
DIALOGUE, AND THE SHARING OF HUMAN, SPIRITUAL AND
MATERIAL RESOURCES WITH ONE ANOTHER.

This formulation of the central "unity" purpose, adopted
by the 1998 assembly in Harare, draws on the experience of
the first fifty years to set out more precisely just what needs
to be involved as the divided churches move towards unity:
prayer, forgiveness, reconciliation, mutual accountability,
deeper relationships, theological dialogue, the sharing of
resources,...

What do we mean by "unity"?
From the beginning the WCC has insisted that it neither
has nor seeks a single, authoritative concept of the proper
unity of the church. It is up to the churches each to pray,
think, discuss and work together with their existing concepts
and approaches. The Council hopes and expects to serve and
encourage them, but never to impose, never to force any
church in a certain direction.

This counters a persistent misconception, summed up in
the term "super-church". Again and again voices have been
raised to object to the WCC as a structure that aims at enforc-
ing its beliefs, practices and priorities on all churches, and to
use the resources of all Christians for goals its leadership will
decide on. This sort of critique was voiced with especial bit-
terness in the early days, against the background of anti-com-
munism in Western countries, by those who supposed the
WCC to be the religious version of a repressive, collectivist,
totalitarian society.

Even if that sort of cold-war rhetoric is seldom heard
today, the "super-church" stereotype has never been completely laid to rest. It tends nowadays to take the form, less
polemically expressed, of a charge that the ecumenical
movement inevitably, if unintentionally, tends to blur the

marvellous variety of Christian expression around the world. This lies, for instance, behind half-humorous references to the WCC as "the Protestant Vatican" – a misleading jibe that overlooks the Orthodox presence.

Yet if the idea of a "super-church" is a serious misconception, it is equally harmful to see membership in the Council as a low-cost way for a church to seem committed to unity while actually spending its time and energies on business as usual. The WCC is equally opposed to being used as an alibi for what its member churches say they want to be doing without actually doing it themselves. The "fellowship of churches" will betray its purposes if anyone treats it as no more than a pleasant club for those taking part in its functions.

Other models

Between these two distortions – overstating the WCC's expectations, or understating its ambitions – lie a range of models of unity with which the fellowship has long been struggling.

We noted in chapter 1 that the unity for which the WCC strives is *visible* unity. To be *visible* the church's unity needs to include: agreement on fundamental theological convictions, especially those on which major churches have split apart; recognition of each other's baptism, and ordained ministry; sharing in each other's eucharist (holy communion, mass, Lord's supper); cooperation in evangelism, witness and service; and a mutually agreed discipline for reaching common decisions. Several of these points are already agreed between certain churches. Yet all too many Christians still differ – and remain separate from one another – because of important differences in faith and practice.

Meetings of the WCC have tried again and again to describe "the unity we seek". In 1937 the Faith and Order conference at Edinburgh spoke of "a church so united that the ultimate loyalty of every member would be given to the whole body and not to any part of it". The WCC's third assembly in New Delhi, 1961, agreed that "God's will and his gift to his church is being made visible as all in each place

Guatemalan refugees in Mexico at worship on Good Friday
Marc van Appelghem

who... confess Jesus Christ as Lord and Saviour are brought by the Holy Spirit into one fully committed fellowship"... (with a long list of related points). The same declaration was insistent that *organic unity* (i.e. that which would grow according to the natural integrity of the body) would not imply "any rigid uniformity of structure, organization or government."

In 1975 the fifth assembly in Nairobi held up the model of "a *conciliar fellowship*" of local churches which are themselves truly united". The visible expression of this would be "councils of representatives of all the local churches at various geographical levels", which would meet to express the mind of the church on issues of faith and life. Again, the goal is not imposed uniformity: the gifts of each member and each local church are to be cherished and protected.

Theologians have suggested other models (for example: unity as *reconciled diversity* or as a *communion of communions*) which place greater emphasis on affirming the legitimacy and value of denominational identities, and the particular contribution each can make in theology, spirituality, devotion and liturgy. These have been discussed in the WCC Faith and Order commission, and found to be less than adequate for the entire, worldwide church.

In a statement on "The Unity of the Church as Koinonia: Gift and Calling", the seventh assembly focused on the *qual-*

ity of the unity the churches are seeking in the WCC, using a Greek word which, as we saw in chapter 2, has ancient ecumenical precedents. "The goal of the search for full communion is realized when *all the churches are able to recognize in one another the one, holy, catholic and apostolic church in its fullness,"* Canberra said. "In such communion churches are bound in all aspects of their life together at all levels in confessing the one faith and engaging in worship and witness, deliberation and action."

This Canberra statement distinguishes between *divisions* by which the church is split apart, and *diversities* in which its different parts happen to differ. In its proclamation of reconciliation, the church works "to overcome divisions based on race, gender, age, culture or colour", which not only damage the credibility of its witness to the world but contradict the nature of the church. At the same time, "diversities which are rooted in theological traditions, various cultural, ethnic or historical contexts are integral to the nature of communion", in which they "are brought together in harmony as gifts of the Holy Spirit".

Theology and practice

Within the WCC it is the Faith and Order commission which concentrates on the theological questions which have in earlier years led to, and still today express, the divisions between churches.

Some churches baptize infants; others administer baptism only to believers who make a public profession of their faith. Some churches have bishops whose consecration to office takes place in a continuity which stretches back to the apostles, others make no fundamental distinction between "laity" and "ordained ministry". Some churches call on the Virgin Mary and other saints in their intercessions; others say this contradicts the unique mediating role of Jesus Christ. Some churches set great store by the affirmation of creeds and confessions; others believe that such formulas restrict the freedom of the individual Christian. Some churches use a wide variety of hymns in their worship; others insist on using only versifications of the Psalms.

In fact, things are often even more complicated. Churches which sing only the Psalms have divided over whether or not it is proper to accompany their singing with musical instruments. Differences over baptism among churches which baptize infants may be as sharp as their quarrels with churches which baptize only believers. Some of the differences which once led to anathemata and excommunications may seem odd or trivial today. Yet at one point in church history they represented something over which Christians felt so strongly as to break fellowship.

To participate in the ecumenical movement is to recognize that these differences arise within "one faith". At the first Faith and Order conference in 1927 the delegates agreed unanimously that "we are united in a common Christian faith which is proclaimed in the holy scriptures and is witnessed to and safeguarded in" the Nicene and Apostles' Creeds and "continuously confirmed in the spiritual experience of the church of Christ". As part of a long-term study of what it can mean for the whole church to confess the apostolic faith today, the Faith and Order commission is now seeking reactions to a text which offers a contemporary ecumenical explication of the Nicene Creed, article by article, phrase by phrase.

To look into some of these doctrinal differences with people of other churches may suggest that they no longer justify the separation to which they once led. In at least two areas already mentioned, discussions in the Faith and Order commission have borne this sort of fruit – the relationship between scripture and Tradition and baptism, eucharist and ministry. By itself, such a conclusion will rarely if ever be enough to heal a division between churches, since the split around the specific point will have been reinforced by other, "non-theological factors". Even so, to reach a better understanding of the point of view of others – and to be obliged to articulate one's own more clearly – may lead to a recognition that barriers to cooperation and fellowship are less formidable than once thought.

Another key factor is that it is seldom enough for theologians and church leaders to come to an understanding of each other's positions, or to agree that a certain formulation adequately expresses a common Christian view of a long-standing area of dispute. It does not follow that the members of their respective churches will immediately share in this convergence. There needs to be a long process of "reception".

The WCC has no authority to proclaim church doctrine, to regulate church order or to initiate steps towards church union. These are matters for the churches themselves. Yet the WCC is ready, if asked, to advise and assist in negotiations towards church union. For as theological discussions of divisive points proceed and the results are communicated to the churches, the hope is that these will be drawn more deeply into working on whatever remaining areas of dispute continue to divide them. One type of forum for doing so has been the "bilateral conversation" in which theologians from two traditions address specific issues in depth. Since the Second Vatican Council (1962-65) the Roman Catholic Church has been much involved with other churches in this kind of exploration.

Called to be a prophetic sign of God's kingdom

Some say that the classic ways of describing church unity focus too much on the churches in themselves, not enough on their witness and service in and for the world. They propose a model of *unity as solidarity*. The decisive division, such people say, is not between denominations but between those in any denomination who believe their faith requires them to challenge injustice in the name of the gospel, or to explore with unbelievers the demands of seeking peace in times of violence, and those who insist that religion is a strictly private affair. Unity will come about as churches stand together publicly in solidarity with the marginalized and in common witness and action against oppression. The sixth assembly at Vancouver in 1983 insisted that "there can be no such division between unity and human renewal, either in the church or in the agenda of the WCC".... "The church is called to be a prophetic 'sign', a prophetic community through which and by which the transformation of the world can take place....

*Above left: Sarah Chakko, India
Above right: Kathleen Bliss, UK
Left: Madeleine Barot, France*
WCC

There never will be a time when the world with all its political, social and economic issues, ceases to be the agenda of the church."

The 1938 decision to bring Faith and Order and Life and Work together to form the WCC was in effect a recognition of the need to integrate these two areas. But the tension between the two continues to affect all levels of the life of the church, not just the WCC.

To construe church unity as solely a matter of overcoming doctrinal differences, disregarding the church's commission to proclaim God's kingdom of justice and reconciliation, is to risk slipping into faith without works. Yet to accent the church's mission in society without regard for confessing the faith that inspires such action is to risk falling into an uncritical activism.

It is precisely in working practically together that a sense of Christian unity can become real and alive. It was lay people and foreign missionaries, working with colleagues of other denominations, who first became aware of the scandal and waste of disunity and who stimulated the beginnings of the ecumenical movement. In recent years, several interchurch bodies originally formed for the practical purpose of coordinating projects of relief and community development have evolved into councils of churches.

Just as different individuals have different gifts and interests, so the different sections of the WCC will have different vocations within the ecumenical movement. The temptation is strong to ignore the importance of facets of the struggle for unity in which one is not involved. The need for mutual correction in holding together "unity in faith and in church order" and "unity in solidarity" remains.

B. [THE CHURCHES THROUGH THE COUNCIL WILL] FACILITATE COMMON WITNESS IN EACH PLACE AND IN ALL PLACES, AND SUPPORT EACH OTHER IN THEIR WORK FOR MISSION AND EVANGELISM.

"You shall be my witnesses" (Acts 1:8) were the final words of the risen Lord to his apostles. The earliest book of church history, the New Testament Acts of the Apostles, is largely a history of evangelism and other facets of the mission Christ entrusted to his church. The central conviction that the church is sent into all the world as the people of God to give testimony to Jesus Christ has been present from the beginning.

The imperative to obedience in the missionary task has also been central to the ecumenical movement since its beginnings in people like Nicolaus von Zinzendorf and William Carey. In the 19th century the story of world mission seemed all too often bound up with the imperialism of European peoples, but in the 20th – not least because of the ecumenical movement – the continuing story has grown in very different ways, and it is set to be different again in the 21st.

"Evangelization is the test of our ecumenical vocation," Philip Potter, the then general secretary of the WCC, told the 1974 world synod of Roman Catholic bishops. The inherent wholeness of witness and unity was explicit already in the final prayer of Jesus before his death when he asked God that his disciples "might be one... so that the world may believe".

In the words of a text on common witness by the Joint Working Group of the WCC and the Roman Catholic Church: "As the church is one body of many members, Christian witness is by its nature communitarian. When one of the faithful acts in individual witness, this is related to the witness of the whole Christian community." It was a "unity" meeting, the 1952 world conference on Faith and Order in Lund, Sweden, that challenged the churches "to act together in all matters except those in which deep differences of conviction compel them to act separately".

In practice, the diversity of Christians making a common witness enables both a better grasp of the situation to which they are speaking and a better hope of communicating with the diversity of people who may be listening. "The peculiar history, tradition and experience which each brings enriches the quality of the common witness," says the WCC-Vatican text. Even when common witness is not possible, for example because of language differences, the witness of a single church is to be seen as a "vicarious way of presenting the witness of other Christians too".

A focal point for reflection and articulation

Since the integration of the International Missionary Council with the WCC in 1961, the WCC has become a focal point for reflecting on the demands of the missionary and evangelistic tasks facing the churches, fed by sharing of information, experiences and insights among the mission agencies, societies and local groups linked to the WCC. Once a decade an intensive assessment of the global mission context is pursued in a world conference on mission and evangelism.

"Mission and Evangelism – An Ecumenical Affirmation" – a brief, summary text drawing on consultations among people involved in mission in WCC member churches, the Roman Catholic Church and other churches not affiliated with the WCC – expresses the heart of the continuing mandate to the whole Christian church: "The church is sent into the world to call people and nations to repentance, to announce forgiveness of sins and a new beginning in relations with God and with neighbours through Jesus Christ."

Over the years since the Edinburgh conference, the experiences of the churches in the ecumenical movement have brought about changes in how they understand this mandate. This search for a deeper understanding has sometimes been painful. The massive thrust of European and North American Christians in the 19th century to bring the gospel to the entire world was often characterized by heroic faith and self-sacrificial devotion. But there was also the shadow side, of links between mission and colonialism, of the export of doctrinal controversies and divisions, of the imposing of Western values and styles of life on people considered uncivilized and unbelieving.

It has proved difficult to learn and even more difficult to put into practice the insight that churches, like the nations in which they live, need to be free from being governed from outside. Or, after "independence", that the external economic domination which remains may be even more effective than political control in denying freedom to churches as to nations. Even within the WCC changes have often come slowly, hindered by the dominance of European languages (especially English) and of the Anglo-Saxon parliamentary style of meetings, which force some people to listen and usually to speak in their second or third language and to participate in an alien way of reaching decisions.

"Sent into the world"

What has this attention to the mission of the church taught Christians about their being "sent into the world"? The *Ecumenical Affirmation* summarizes its "ecumenical perception of Christian mission" under seven headings. These sections provide stimulating material for Christians in many different situations to think through for their part in the worldwide missionary and evangelistic task.

Conversion: "The proclamation of the gospel includes an invitation to recognize and accept in a personal decision the saving lordship of Christ. It is the announcement of a personal encounter, mediated by the Holy Spirit, with the living Christ, receiving his forgiveness and making a personal acceptance of the call to discipleship and a life of service." This call comes alike to individuals and to nations, groups and families, appealing to all to turn away from war, injustice, racism and hatred.

The gospel to all realms of life: Witness is proclaiming Christ as Lord over all life, not just over one's personal beliefs and spirituality. The church claims "the right and the duty to address itself openly to issues of human concern." Today, for example, it is called to witness in the area of science and technology, not only by offering ethical guidance, but also by raising theological questions about the meaning of human existence and the goal of history. Announcing such an all-embracing gospel may involve denouncing powers of sin and injustice, who in turn may restrict Christian witness or repress and even persecute those offering it.

Mission in Christ's way: The gospel is either illustrated or betrayed by how it is announced to people. In all cases power must be subordinate to love. Effective mission is often unspectacular, carried out by "unsensational people who gather together steadfastly in small, caring communities whose life prompts the question: "What is the source of the meaning of your life? What is the power of your powerlessness?", giving the occasion to name the Name."

The church and unity in God's mission: Divisions among the churches, who cannot all join in the eucharist, given by

Christ as "bread for missionary people", affect the credibility of Christian witness. "Many who are attracted to the vision of the kingdom find it difficult to be attracted to the concrete reality of the church."

Called to unity in mission, churches must plant the seed of the good news everywhere, "until there is, in every human community, a cell of the kingdom, a church confessing Jesus Christ and in his name serving his people". To plant the church in different communities requires Christians to "express their faith in the symbols and images of their respective culture". The resulting cultural diversity may create tensions, but "the unity we look for is not uniformity but the multiple expression of a common faith and a common mission".

Good news to the poor: The number of materially poor and marginalized people in the world is steadily increasing. Many have never had the gospel presented to them in a way they can recognize as good news. "This is a double injustice: they are victims of the oppression of an unjust economic order or an unjust political distribution of power, and at the same time they are deprived of the knowledge of God's special care for them."

The proclamation of the gospel among the poor is the criterion for judging the validity of missionary engagement. God's "preferential option for the poor" is the yardstick by which to measure "our lives as individual Christians, local congregations and as missionary people of God in the world".

But what does this mean for the non-poor? "God wants all human beings to be saved and to come to the knowledge of truth, but we know that while God's purpose is universal, his action is always particular. What we are learning anew today is that God works through the downtrodden, the persecuted, the poor of the earth. And from there, he is calling all humanity to follow him. For all of us, the invitation is clear: to follow Jesus in identification and sharing with the weak, marginalized and poor of the world, because in them we encounter him."

Mission in and to six continents: Seeing mission ecumenically means abandoning the old distinction between "sending" and "receiving" churches. In what were once called "Christian countries", churches have lost touch with workers, youth and many others. At the same time, migrants and refugees bring the missionary frontier "to the doorstep of every parish". If what a church says about global mission is to be credible, it must demonstrate "a serious missionary engagement at home".

Does giving priority to congregation-based mission in its own setting mean the end of "mission across frontiers"? A temporary or permanent halt to sending and receiving missionaries and resources across national boundaries – to encourage recovery of the identity of every church – "does not mean the end of the missionary vocation nor of the duty to provide resources for missionary work, but it does mean freedom to reconsider present engagements and to see whether a continuation of what we have been doing for so long is the right style of mission in our day."

There will always be a need for people who are called and equipped to cross frontiers to share the gospel, but their special calling is no substitute for the missionary vocation of the entire church in and for every place.

Witness among people of living faiths: "In Jesus of Nazareth the Word became a true human being. The wonder of his ministry of love persuades Christians to testify to people of every religious and non-religious persuasion of this decisive presence of God in Christ. In him is our salvation." But how do Christians fulfil their missionary obligation in the context of neighbours who live by other religious and ideological persuasions? There are deep differences within the ecumenical community on how "salvation in Christ is available to people of diverse religious persuasions". But all agree that witness should be rendered to all.

"Such an attitude springs from the assurance that God is the creator of the whole universe and that he has not left himself without witness at any time or in any place. The Spirit of God is constantly at work in ways that pass human understanding and in places that are to us least expected. In entering into a relationship of dialogue with others, therefore, Christians seek to discern the unsearchable riches of God and the way he deals with humanity.

"Life with people of other faiths and ideologies is an encounter of commitments. Witness cannot be a one-way process, but of necessity is two-way; in it Christians become aware of some of the deepest convictions of their neighbours" and, "within a spirit of openness and trust are able to bear authentic witness, giving an account of their commitment to the Christ who calls all persons to himself".

We shall look further into the WCC's involvements with people of other faiths in the next chapter (see p. 132-37).

C. [THE CHURCHES THROUGH THE COUNCIL WILL] EXPRESS THEIR COMMITMENT TO DIAKONIA IN SERVING HUMAN NEED, BREAKING DOWN BARRIERS BETWEEN PEOPLE, PROMOTING ONE HUMAN FAMILY IN JUSTICE AND PEACE, AND UPHOLDING THE INTEGRITY OF CREATION, SO THAT ALL MAY EXPERIENCE THE FULLNESS OF LIFE.

That diakonia, the service of human need, will always deserve a high place on the churches' agenda cannot be called in question. The interminable chronicle of human tragedies brought into our homes each day by the mass media is a constant call to Christian hearts and consciences. So also the desirability that such service shall be known to be given in the name of the whole church, not just one part, is of key importance in and to the ecumenical movement.

Nonetheless, despite the substantial sharing the member churches already undertake through the WCC, the Council's responsibilities in this field represent a very small part of the total aid given by Christians. Precise statistics are virtually impossible to establish, but the best estimates are that the value of what is channelled through the WCC is no more than five to ten percent of the whole. The WCC does not seek a monopoly on interchurch aid; its concern is simply that assistance be given in such a way that the most urgent needs of the greatest number of the most needy people are met, and that bilateral giving (i.e. between Christians of the same confessional or denominational tradition) and independent Christian charity not be given with conditions that reinforce structures of domination or dependence.

The many faces of ecumenical diakonia

Christian service probably has its highest profile in *emergency relief*. Since disasters often elicit immediate material aid from many quarters – governments, United Nations bodies, the Red Cross and major non-governmental agencies –

The WCC and the Lutheran World Federation distribute mattresses to Palestinian refugees in UN Relief and Works Agency emergency camps in June 1967 UNRWA

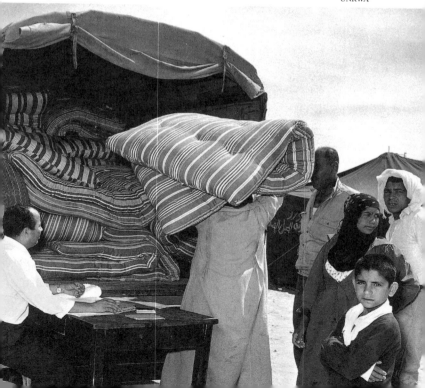

the churches locally and internationally try not to duplicate those contributions but rather to identify their specific role in the overall relief effort. Since 1995 the WCC and the Lutheran World Federation have been working together to coordinate emergency response through a network of churches and church agencies known as Action of Churches Together (ACT). Yet, ACT has noted, there are many situations where "the churches themselves are not strong, so that ACT's ability to take the lead in humanitarian action is diminished".

Besides meeting immediate material needs, the churches have a pastoral task, responding to the shock and sorrow of the victims, and an advocacy role, seeing that the aid available does not pass by the most neglected. Not all human misery is the consequence of a disaster; and aid sent to alleviate suffering may in fact be used to work against addressing and removing the causes of that suffering. Effective diakonia by the Christian community must go beyond "mere" charity.

Development as the new name for peace

The ecumenical movement and many churches threw much of their diaconal effort in the 1960s and 1970s into development, especially in the newly independent countries. Development agencies became large organizations in the wealthier countries, and powerful forces in the poorer, with contributions from church members sometimes supplemented by substantial funding from governments.

The WCC's own programme of interchurch aid evolved accordingly, building on principles set down in the early years, emphasizing the priority of assistance that could reach the neediest people and which did not simply follow denominational or confessional lines. The WCC, with a few exceptions, has never operated or staffed these projects for development itself; its role is that of channelling resources and strengthening the capacities of churches to put such resources to effective use.

Already in the 1980s, optimism about development was waning. Awareness was growing that, despite sizeable investment in development projects, the churches and the vulnerable people they sought to aid were losing the struggle for justice. A major consultation in 1986 suggested that an approach focusing on projects for development should give way to an area-centred approach.

By continuously enlarging and deepening awareness of the political, social, economic and church situation in each area, the total Christian community could respond more effectively to the range of needs, and entrust to the churches in those areas the prime responsibility for initiating and overseeing what could and should be done in the name of the whole church. In contrast to the earlier process of *reacting* by responding to requests for support for appropriate projects – often slowly by the time all the procedures were followed – an area-centred approach would enable the churches to *act* more quickly and creatively.

So support for particular actions could come in the context of an overall approach incorporating a long-range concern for the area, the sharing of information, advocacy for victims of injustice, theological reflection, pastoral care and development of human resources. A central – and ecumenically challenging – conviction of this vision of a more comprehensive and more prophetic diakonia is that the local churches must be granted, indeed must take, more immediate responsibility for the service of the whole church in and for the poor in their area.

Refugees

Even if insights into service to people in need have evolved in the ecumenical community over the years, the kinds of pain and suffering that call for diakonia today are often similar to those of forty or fifty years ago. Refugee service is a case in point. The second world war left 12 million people homeless in Europe alone. Within a short time a new refugee situation arose with the partition of Palestine and the creation of the state of Israel. In the following decades, the many famines and the civil wars, the periods of racial or religious strife, made millions of people elsewhere

refugees too, particularly in Africa, Central America and Southeast Asia.

Meanwhile a new challenge to the churches' service to the displaced grew up in Western Europe with the growing population of migrant workers. Ecumenical refugee services had to face new obstacles, as fear of foreigners and changing economic circumstances even in apparently wealthy countries led those who once boasted of openness to those seeking refuge to allow ever fewer asylum-seekers in, and to restrict the openings to work, residence or money, for those who did manage to enter.

The Ecumenical Church Loan Fund

One instrument of the international Christian community which has adapted to changing circumstances is the Ecumenical Church Loan Fund (ECLOF). It was created in 1946 in response to the need to replace thousands of destroyed church buildings in Europe. By the end of the 1960s this need had largely been met, so ECLOF shifted its focus to lending money to help people "damaged by economic underdevelopment, social injustice and oppression". Using donated capital, the fund now lends money to national ECLOF committees at low interest with no specific repayment period. The national committees in turn screen requests from and make loans in local currency to grassroots organizations. These loans are repaid within a set period, thus converting the capital into a revolving fund for more loans.

Health and healing

In the 19th-century missionary movement, doctors and nurses often accompanied evangelists, preachers and teachers, so that clinics and hospitals were frequently built alongside churches and schools. By the 1960s the end of colonialism had led to a crisis in medical mission, for many new nations were placing responsibility for health care on their governments. The WCC called a consultation in 1964 to explore this situation. On the basis of its declaration about a Christian understanding of healing and the acknowledged

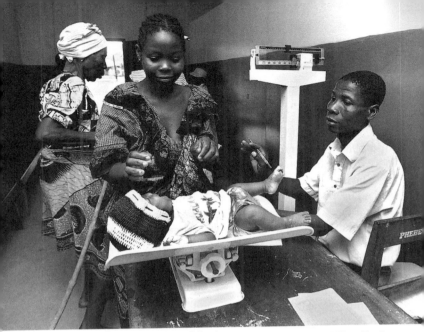

Phebe hospital in northern Liberia   WCC/Jonas Ekströmer

need for help from the wider Christian community for churches seeking to put these new insights into action, the WCC began to help churches in those countries establish their own national coordinating agencies for health care. Emphasis has been given to community-based primary health care as an alternative to increasingly sophisticated and expensive medical technology, inaccessible to most people in the world.

Justice and peace

The link between "ministering to human need" and "the promotion of one human family in justice and peace" has put questions of economic power on the ecumenical agenda since the 1920s. Significant economic analysis and forthright statements about social evils were made by the Stockholm conference on Life and Work in 1925 and the Oxford conference on "Church, Community and State" in 1937.

At its founding assembly the WCC began to explore the meaning of a "responsible society", and took this further in the 1960s by looking into the churches' role in situations of "rapid social change". That led in the 1970s to examination of world economic systems. Along with other agencies, the WCC has engaged in critical studies of transnational corporations, the global financial system and – especially since the mid-1980s – the crisis caused by the external debt of many poor countries.

Statements about economic matters are often controversial. The WCC's studies of economic powers have challenged the source of the wealth of many churches and their members; and much of this discussion of the positive and negative aspects of capitalism and socialism was carried on in the shadow of the cold war.

Racial equality

Similar tensions have surrounded other aspects of the WCC's efforts to "promote one human family in justice and peace". Even if few people would call that goal in question, support for particular strategies and proposals to achieve it may arouse disagreement both within and beyond the Christian community.

The most obvious example of this has been the struggle against racism. In the previous chapter it was mentioned that the WCC's Programme to Combat Racism (PCR) was formed out of a conviction that the victims of racism must undertake their own liberation; outsiders can play only supporting roles. Yet bitter disagreements have arisen when that support took the form of grants from the Special Fund of the PCR to organizations engaged in armed struggle – the liberation movements fighting for an end to white-minority rule in Mozambique, Angola, Zimbabwe (then Rhodesia), Namibia (then South-West Africa), and South Africa.

Since it was church money, those movements undertook to spend any such grants for humanitarian purposes, while the WCC insisted that the money was given "without control of the manner in which it is to be spent", since it saw the trust involved as essential to the solidarity with the victims of racial injustice which the grants were intended to express. Nevertheless, the accusation was often made that the WCC was "buying guns for guerrillas".

Many more, even among those who are aware that there has never been any evidence for that accusation, have still expressed unease or outright opposition to church financing for such organizations. The fact that only money specifically designated for that Special Fund – and thus no general WCC money – is used for the grants was not enough to quiet that unease. The opponents were not impressed either by the observation that the size of the grants could hardly make a significant contribution to the buying of costly modern weapons. They contended that the decision of a liberation movement to take up arms to achieve its goals should make it ineligible for any church support, no matter what the money was used for and no matter how worthy those goals.

In the long history of the church, refusal to support war has been the exception rather than the rule. So there is an inconsistency in the arguments just mentioned when they are made by those who do not profess a commitment to pacifism – especially if their nation has enjoyed the benefits of independence ensured by victory in war. Yet these debates have ensured that the ecumenical movement has had to take seri-

"No money for apartheid" say these protesters in Frankfurt, one of 70 cities in Germany which witnessed similar actions in 1988

EPD-bild/Müller

ously the question of violence not just as a debating point but as an unresolved issue. It has pondered the example of Jesus, the biblical witnesses, the lessons of church history, the relation of ends to means, and the new challenges of modern weapons.

Some ecumenical convergences have appeared. One is that violence will often take silent or structured form, so that churches which support the status quo may be giving unrecognized legitimacy to the powers imposing that violence. There is now a widespread recognition that in extreme cases the oppressed may be forced into the use of arms by the refusal of a violent, oppressive regime to allow them recourse to peaceful means of righting wrongs. In a 1973 declaration on violence and non-violence the WCC warned against dictating "strategies and tactics to people living in distant and different situations". Those outside must recall that "it is not they, but others, who will be called upon to pay the price".

Above all the WCC has held before all Christians the imperative of working for *justice and reconciliation*. Hence its insistence, in Southern Africa, on economic sanctions and disinvestment as peaceful means to end the injustices of apartheid. Hence too its challenge to Christians who reject all use of violence to take onto their own shoulders the sufferings of the oppressed, and to acknowledge a responsibility for removing the structures of oppression. On a recommendation of the Harare assembly (1998), the WCC has proclaimed the period 2001-2010 a Decade to Overcome Violence: Churches Seeking Reconciliation and Peace. It is the intention of the decade to engage the churches in the promotion and support of non-violent, peaceful ways of resolving conflict.

Nuclear weapons

Nuclear weapons are another source of debate in the ecumenical movement. For half a century unanimous recognition of the apocalyptic dimensions of such weapons has not brought agreement about what should be done with those which already exist. Some voices argue pragmatically that the policy of deterrence has prevented the use of nuclear weapons since 1945. Others contend that nuclear weapons are inherently immoral because their deterrent value depends on a willingness to entertain conditions under which their possessors could use them.

Christians from the Pacific Islands dispute the claim that there have been no victims of nuclear weapons since August 1945. Hundreds of nuclear tests in the Marshall Islands and French Polynesia have left a legacy of radiation, related diseases, uninhabitable land, damage to a fragile environment and fears fed by the fact that data about the consequences on human health of nuclear testing a generation ago are still kept secret.

Especially Christians from the South have stressed that preoccupation with nuclear disarmament breaks the essential link between peace and justice that pervades the writings of the Old Testament prophets. For the majority of the earth's population, the most immediate threat to survival has never been posed by nuclear weapons, but by the oppression, poverty, homelessness and starvation which have spread even while governments devote astronomical sums to ever more destructive armaments in the vain pursuit of "national security".

Pacifist Christians have argued that the dispute about nuclear weapons is merely a corollary of a larger unsettled item on the ecumenical social agenda – the Christian attitude towards war. In the shadow of the second world war, the Amsterdam assembly declared that "war is contrary to the will of God". Yet more than fifty years of discussing war, during which millions have lost their lives in "limited" wars, have failed to sharpen this rejection of war into more specific or binding ethical guidance.

The increasing destructiveness of conventional weapons has made this discussion a matter of urgency. The Canberra assembly wrestled at length with this in its debate about the Gulf War in February 1991. The WCC, other ecumenical organizations and many individual churches had gone on record in opposition to a military effort to remove Iraqi troops from Kuwait. The assembly, meeting just as the air assault on Iraq and its forces in Kuwait reached its height, adopted a text which called on the churches "to give up any theological or moral justification of the use of military power, be it in war or through other forms of oppressive security systems, and become public advocates of a just peace". Yet when some delegates later protested that this would in effect be a declaration by the WCC of a pacifist position, the assembly decided to withdraw these words and bypass any general discussion of the permissibility of war as such, in favour of a text addressing only the actual war going on at that moment.

Especially perhaps for Christians in the North, the destructiveness and suffering caused by the Gulf War and its aftermath was a sobering reminder that the end of the cold war had done little to lessen the urgency for the churches to engage in a ministry of peace-making and reconciliation. On the contrary, the radically new situations in Central and Eastern Europe and the former Soviet Union at the end of the century brought harsh reminders of the potential in long-suppressed ethnic conflicts for causing suffering and devastation, all too often aggravated by religious differences.

The role of the United Nations

Another area of concern, in the context of "one human family", where the enthusiasm of the immediate post-second world war years has given way to a more sober commitment is that of the churches' relationship with the United Nations.

This relationship was hailed in the earlier assemblies as a great new step forward, with a WCC team closely involved in the drafting of the 1948 UN Universal Declaration of Human Rights, with messages sent to each successive assembly by the secretary-general of the UN. Speakers at the 1968 Uppsala assembly immediately involved in UN affairs included President Kenneth Kaunda of Zambia, Lord Hugh Caradon (UK representative to the UN) and Robert Gardiner (of Ghana, secretary of the UN Economic Commission for Africa). But the mood by the end of the century has become less upbeat, with general awareness that the UN has to struggle for its place in international affairs no less than such bodies as the WCC.

Nonetheless, the WCC central committee at its last meeting of the century in 1999, in the shadow of the Kosovo campaign, reaffirmed "the WCC's conviction that the UN is the unique instrument of the peoples of the world for guaranteeing respect for the international rule of law". The committee urged that the WCC pursue a study of the ethics of humanitarian intervention, "taking into account the legitimate right of states to be free of undue interference in their internal affairs and the moral obligation of the international community to respond when states are unwilling or incapable of guaranteeing respect for human rights and peace within their own borders". The preliminary results of this study were received by the central committee in 2001 and published as a study document: "The Protection of Endangered Populations in Situations of Armed Violence".

Human rights

Ever since the Commission of the Churches on International Affairs played an active part in 1948 in drafting the section on "religious liberty" of the Universal Declaration of Human Rights, the WCC has continued to follow closely – and at times itself offer a lead – in the development of the world's commitment to human rights.

Information from member churches and related organizations enables the Council to monitor situations in which people's rights are violated. While the primary responsibility for advocacy in these situations belongs to the local churches, the WCC may – if international ecumenical intervention is likely to be helpful – intercede with authorities on behalf of victims. In Latin America in the 1960s and 1970s the WCC provided resources for regional efforts, when defending human rights there was a high priority – and a great risk – for churches under military dictatorships.

Mothers of the "disappeared" in the Plaza de Mayo in Buenos Aires, Argentina

Western European and North American churches shaped the original stance of the WCC on human rights. Deeply rooted in their traditions was the notion of "freedom rights", the obligation of a state and its citizens to refrain from interfering with an individual's "pursuit of happiness" (as the US declaration of Independence phrased it). The right to freedom of religion drew the WCC's closest attention.

But as more and more newly independent, former mission churches in newly independent countries joined the Council, they suggested that non-interference by governments is too narrow a concept. The ability of the powerful to oppress the weak is built into many systems of injustice. A new strategy for defining human rights was required.

So the WCC's fifth assembly in Nairobi in 1975 reflected this broader approach in enumerating a list of human rights which include guarantees of life, self-determination, cultural identity, rights of minorities, participation in decision-making within one's own community, dissent, personal dignity and religious freedom. In 1998, the eighth assembly in Harare approved both a strong reaffirmation of the 1948 Universal Declaration and a new statement of its own identifying 19 areas of human rights that deserve to be as universal as those listed in 1948. These include elimination of the death penalty, rights of women, rights of uprooted people, rights of indigenous peoples and rights of people with disabilities.

Dissenters in European countries under Soviet domination

One area where the WCC has come under sustained criticism in certain quarters has been its behaviour in relation to the forty years of Soviet domination of Central and Eastern Europe. Was the Council guilty of "selective indignation" in speaking out about injustices in, say, South Africa or Chile, but not in Czechoslovakia or the USSR?

It may be helpful to summarize a significant conversation which WCC general secretary Konrad Raiser was able to have in 1999 in the Czech Republic with ten persons who had been involved in a dissident network within the Evangelical Church of Czech Brethren (a founding member church) during the years of cold war. They reproached the WCC (a) that its efforts during those years to hold together the churches of East and West Europe had not allowed space for a free dialogue within the churches; (b) that the WCC's concentration on injustice in the third world diminished its capacity to analyze and publicize the comparable issues in their countries; and (c) that the WCC's focus on relations with official church institutions made the communist governments censors of ecumenical relationships.

Raiser acknowledged that the Council had failed to take as seriously as they deserved such dissident initiatives. Its efforts to contact and support them had been too limited and hidden. Yet he pointed out that some of the disagreements, at the time and still today, reflect divergences in interpretation of the situation as a whole, as well as divergences in ethical or political assessment of what could be done. What is important now, said Raiser, is "for all voices to be heard, and for this often painful history to be revisited together".

Over its fifty and more years, the WCC has become aware that *public statements* are an effective method of action only in certain situations. Speaking out about an initiative in a totalitarian country, where the mass media are government controlled and a critical statement from outside will never be heard by the people, may prove counter-productive. It can lead to greater restriction or oppression of the church without any change by the government. It was often this caution, rather than any ideological bias, that explains the differences of expectation in different situations.

As a council of churches, the WCC's main responsibility is to help the churches in each local situation proclaim the gospel of justice, peace and reconciliation. Helping an individual church follow Jesus Christ may sometimes mean forcefully denouncing the actions of the government of its country. At other times, it will mean silently suffering with a church in its predicament, out of sensitivity to the plight of Christians or to inter-religious peace in that country. The central issues are the welfare of the people and the safety of the church. Statements from the WCC and other outsiders are made not in order to score ideological points or to vent indignation, but to support suffering people and to encourage those who can to work sensitively to change the situation.

D. [THE CHURCHES THROUGH THE COUNCIL WILL] NURTURE
THE GROWTH OF AN ECUMENICAL CONSCIOUSNESS THROUGH
PROCESSES OF EDUCATION AND A VISION OF LIFE IN COMMU-
NITY ROOTED IN EACH PARTICULAR CULTURAL CONTEXT.

Education for life-long learning

"An ecumenical consciousness" is a big phrase, pointing
in a myriad of directions. Yet anyone coming into contact
with the ecumenical movement will immediately realize not
only what a lot he or she has to learn – about other churches,
other cultures and life-styles, other areas of common concern
than those that she or he already knows about – but also how
liberating and exciting it is to be part of a community of
learning in Christ's name. So it is not surprising that many
different aspects of the WCC's work have strong educational
components.

The roots of the education programmes that the WCC
inherited from the World Council of Christian Education,
chiefly supporting *Sunday school* and other programmes
directly run by churches for their members, can be traced
back to beginnings in the last years of the 18th century. Yet
the educational ministry of the church is far older than that;
already in the early church the preparation of candidates for
baptism was an important priority, and in the middle ages
monasteries of the Middle East and Europe were the chief
providers of literacy and teaching in the human and natural
sciences.

In the later 20th century the WCC has needed to be no
less aware of the potential Christian contributions to the vast
range of educational programmes undertaken by governments and a host of other agencies in virtually all countries.
Its small education office cannot begin to be directly
involved in each and every facet of all this, but by making the
most of the Council's consultative relationship to UNESCO
and other world educational bodies, it is very much part of
that office's task to be both learning about developments in
education around the world and to feed in to those secular
agencies the best Christian thought on education.

The wide range of languages and cultures among member churches makes it impossible for the WCC to be involved directly in the production of curricula and study materials, or in teacher training. The Council's role, as on many other matters, is chiefly an enabling and encouraging one, challenging churches to recognize the importance and practical advantages of exposing their members to the experiences, gifts and needs of Christians living in very different circumstances.

Students at one of five clergy training centres of the Ethiopian Orthodox Church receive ministerial training that focuses on promoting self-reliance in congregations and communities across the country

Two WCC staff members who have made a memorable personal contribution through education are Paulo Freire of Brazil and Hans-Ruedi Weber of Switzerland and Indonesia. Freire served in the WCC in the 1970s after a stormy period of pioneering literacy and – through that – political education in his home country. He showed how "conscientization" (making people aware) was a key element in the liberation for which so many in Latin America were longing. By his books and example, he set a generation of teachers working in down-to-earth ways with people previously judged ineducable.

Hans-Ruedi Weber served in the WCC first as secretary for the Laity in the 1960s, then as an educator in the Council's Bossey Institute, and in the 1980s as secretary for Bible study. He led seminars in many countries and published a series of books using art from many cultures to develop ways to open up study of the Bible for people who had never seen that as something they could themselves do. Here he followed in the footsteps, a generation earlier, of Suzanne de Diétrich of France, whose *Rediscovery of the Bible* had a key influence on the early leaders of the WCC. Knowing the word of God that speaks through the scriptures remains a key resource of the ecumenical movement.

Direct educational assistance to individuals comes through the WCC scholarships programme. National committees recommend candidates for study abroad in many different academic and practical fields. In recent years scholarships have been awarded annually to some 200 people, coming from many different churches and countries and studying in cultures and languages other than their own. The WCC scholarships office helps churches put forward candidates whose education will serve the needs of the church, not just their personal advancement.

Many seminaries and theological colleges have received aid from the *Theological Education Fund*. This was set up by the International Missionary Council in 1958, integrated into the WCC with the IMC in the 1960s and transformed into the Programme for Theological Education in the 1980s. While funds are still channelled to theological institutions, the Council's involvement in the churches' concern for training for ministry, by lay and ordained, has widened; the Council has seen its Ecumenical Institute in Bossey as a laboratory for this.

The fundamental convictions are two: (a) that theology and ministry must be "by the people", and not just the speciality of academically trained professionals; and (b) that theological education will best serve when it is both intended for the whole church and concerned to encourage the search for the wholeness of the church in and for the whole human family.

While Christian scholars in many disciplines now expect to work in collaboration with colleagues from different churches as a matter of course, the academic study of the ecumenical movement as a particular discipline has dwindled in some countries. Many seminaries have no specific place in the curriculum for it. This means fewer clergy will be acquainted with the movement, which is bound to have consequences for the priority given to the ecumenical vision in their churches.

Worshipping in the ecumenical community

Worship, no less than education, has always been central to the life of the Christian church. Thought about it has in many areas developed enormously in the 20th century. Theological studies of the nature of worship in the early part of the century, mostly within the separate traditions, provided a key background for renewal of many sorts in mid-century.

In the early years of the WCC, worship followed closely the practices and customs of the individual churches, so that each assembly enabled its participants to worship in the traditions of several of the major confessions. Starting with the Vancouver assembly in 1983, the WCC has developed a fresh approach to worship – drawing inspiration from Taizé, Iona and others.

One feature has been to hold assembly worship in a huge tent, whose open sides constantly remind everyone that this worship is not just for those who are present but is "for the world". Still more, the way chants and songs, pictures and banners, gestures and prayer forms taken from many different cultures and backgrounds can be shaped into acts of participatory worship for that particular community in that specific time and place, is proving an inspiration for local churches and meetings all over the world.

Despite this potential for enhanced participation and renewal, to share in worship within the ecumenical community is by no means a panacea. For it is also in the context of worship – throughout the life of the WCC – that one of the most painful evidences of the divisions between churches becomes apparent, namely the impossibility of all churches joining together in "the one eucharistic fellowship". No way of resolving the central disagreement has yet been discovered: is the Lord's supper a "means of moving into unity" or the expression of a "unity already given"? The sight of Christians whose conscience makes it impossible for them to share in the celebration with their sisters and brothers of other churches reminds everyone of the distance we still have to go on the way to church unity.

E. [THE CHURCHES THROUGH THE COUNCIL WILL] ASSIST EACH OTHER IN THEIR RELATIONSHIPS TO AND WITH PEOPLE OF OTHER FAITH COMMUNITIES.

This is a relatively recent addition to the Council's goals, one that was heatedly debated in the 1970s, and yet which has become one of the WCC's greatest services, not just to its member churches but to religious relationships in all continents.

Already the world missionary conference at Edinburgh in 1910 was aware of the importance of good relationships between Christians, and people of other faiths. A set of 11 leading questions were sent to a cross-section of missionaries, and 187 responses were received. But the first world war made it impossible to follow up the commission report to the conference directly.

Amman, Jordan

However, the IMC never lost sight of this area of concern. Both its interwar conferences, in Jerusalem in 1928 where attention was also given to "the secular", and in Tambaram in 1938 for which Hendrik Kraemer wrote *The Christian Message in a Non-Christian World*, struggled over this topic. At the time of integration with the WCC a study was under way on "The Word of God and the Living Faiths of Men", pursued as a study by Christian theologians for the wider Christian community.

A breakthrough came in the late 1960s, with the appointment of Stanley Samartha, from India, as secretary for interfaith relationships. His first efforts led to the realization that what is crucial is the dialogue between actual persons as persons; it is never "faiths" that meet or conflict, only persons. So the programme was named Dialogue between People of Living Faiths.

"It is the grace of God that draws us out of isolation into genuine dialogue with other people," said the report from one of the first meetings in that programme. Such confidence in the positive results of meeting was questioned, at times sharply, in the 1975 Nairobi assembly. But the consensus remained that for all the unanswerable questions the commitment to meeting, sharing and discovering more from one another should be sustained. By the end of the century the WCC's lead in this, alongside comparable efforts by Pope

John Paul II and others, has encouraged a flood of initiatives at local and national levels.

F. [THE CHURCHES THROUGH THE COUNCIL WILL] FOSTER RENEWAL AND GROWTH IN UNITY, WORSHIP, MISSION AND SERVICE.

This final clause of the 1998 Constitution's statement of purposes and functions is a catch-all; unity, worship, mission and service have already figured at length in this chapter. Yet the stress on "renewal" in and through each of those is no mere word. The 1947 letter inviting churches to the founding assembly in Amsterdam acknowledged that the horrors of the war just ended had to be seen as due in part to the failures of the churches. "Our first and deepest need", that letter said, "is not new organization, but the renewal, or rather the rebirth, of the actual churches."

Within the ecumenical movement, renewal is not seen as a matter only for the churches. Renewal is the creative work of God in which a repentant people rediscover their identity, are freed from entangling alliances with worldly powers, and are rebuilt by the Holy Spirit into a fit community for modelling God's purposes for the total human family.

So one way the WCC has served the renewal of all churches has been the emphasis it has placed on the participation of representatives of the "whole people of God" in the work and decision-making of the churches.

The laity: One focal point of the concern for renewal, especially in the early years of the Council, was the distinctive ministry of the laity. Joseph Oldham wrote that Christian witness in social and political life must be made "by the action of the multitude of Christian men and women who are actively engaged from day to day in the conduct of administration, industry and the affairs of the public and common life". The ministry of the laity is built on an awareness of the church as the people of God (the Greek word *laos*, from which "laity" is derived, means "people").

Beside being a logical outgrowth of the concern for committed and competent intervention in social and political matters, this accent on the renewing potential of an active and engaged laity was strengthened by the role unordained people played in many European parishes during the wartime shortage of pastors. The WCC's Ecumenical Institute in Bossey was founded with the vision of equipping lay people for effective Christian presence in the world, though after the growth of lay academies, above all in Germany, and of similar study centres around the world, its emphasis shifted to ecumenical theological training. The WCC maintains contacts with a worldwide network of lay and study centres, and periodically organizes meetings of representatives of these.

Women: From its beginnings the WCC has stressed that to know the church as the whole people of God will mean giving attention to the role of women. As already noted, wartime experiences helped to put this concern on the agenda of the Amsterdam assembly, with the documentation of women's contributions to the churches as a basis for the WCC's early programmes in this area.

The accent has fallen throughout on *the partnership of women and men* in the church, working out Paul's vision in Galatians 3:28 that in Christ Jesus "there is neither Jew nor Greek... slave nor free... male nor female". To be sure, the churches' practice falls short of this idea. Even where women played roles beyond those they have in society, few if any positions of leadership were open to them. The WCC's study on the "Community of Women and Men in the Church" that culminated in a 1981 conference in Sheffield, UK, is widely remembered for advocating an increase of opportunities for women.

Since that time, there has also been growing attention in the WCC and its member churches to women's theology. An increasing number of churches have debated the question whether women may be ordained to the pastoral ministry. Voices of Christian feminists have become more influential. There has been a new interest in how women read the Bible and pursue theological issues in ways distinct from those of men. Still more, the Decade of Churches in Solidarity with Women, which the WCC launched in 1988 in the light of the disappointing results of the earlier UN Decade of Women, while it largely failed to alter the overall priorities of the churches, succeeded in heightening the profile of women's activities in many churches and in the WCC. In particular, the mid-Decade visits paid by international teams to 330 member churches brought to the fore issues of the violence inflicted on women and of the barriers to effective participation by women in many societies and churches.

With member churches rooted in different confessions and cultures, the WCC remains a forum for facing tensions in this area. Moreover, the Council's efforts to reflect the equality of women and men, which all churches accept in principle, are hampered by the realities in the life of the member churches. Finding women executive staff for the WCC, for example, depends on the availability of women who have had appropriate experience and have developed the necessary skills in their own home settings. Again, while the Council can encourage and suggest a certain level of representation for women in delegations to its assemblies and other gatherings it cannot force the churches to meet that level.

Yet it must be emphasized that the Council's concern with the community of women and men reaches well beyond church life. The greater vulnerability of women to poverty, injustice and suffering, has been documented repeatedly. The empowerment of women in rural areas has been a frequent emphasis in development programmes. Wider accessibility of education for girls and women has been shown to be one of the most crucial factors alike for economic growth and for social health in any society.

Young people: The enthusiasm and intelligence of students and other young people gave a decisive impetus to the early stages of the ecumenical movement. Bodies which brought together youth from different countries and confessions – particularly the World Student Christian Federation – proved to be the crucible of the new movement. Many leaders of the WCC in its first stages had their first ecumenical experiences in local and national Student Christian Movement chapters.

So from the outset it was insisted that the perspectives of young people belong in the Council not just because youth are "the church of the future" but because they already have full membership in the body of Christ. Yet, as more than 300

A presentation on International Youth Year at the WCC's central committee meeting in Buenos Aires (1985)

participants in a youth event leading up to the 1991 Canberra assembly noted in their message, "as young people, and especially young women, we are often deprived of freedom by our churches, which render us voiceless, powerless and marginalized in the name of "experience" and "knowledge". Nonetheless, they went on, "as young people we feel the greatest burden of human rights abuses, of economic and social injustice, of apartheid, of civil and international war and other forms of corporate evil".

The voice of youth is seldom a comfortable one for older leaders to hear; and of course the youth constituency is always changing – no one remains a young person, even by the broad definition accepted within the WCC, for more than a decade or so.

Much early youth work in the WCC concentrated on work camps for the rebuilding of Europe following the war; later these were taken up on a smaller scale in other parts of the world. The Council also helped to channel start-up funds to a number of small youth-related projects and programmes. In more recent years, WCC work with young people has focused on helping local, national and regional youth movements build a global constituency around the priorities of spirituality, justice, peace and the integrity of creation. In 1993 the Council organized an Ecumenical Global Gathering of Youth and Students in Brazil, as a new point of departure for youth initiatives.

Young people have travelled to different countries in groups under WCC sponsorship, and short-term internships have been arranged across regions. Each major WCC conference and assembly brings young people from many backgrounds to serve as stewards, providing practical services while making new friends and learning about the ecumenical movement.

Obstacles to renewal: Despite the degree of agreement and engagement achieved by these emphases on education and worship, on the roles of lay people, women and the young, these aspects of the WCC's life and work are often eclipsed – in regard to public attention and specific funding – by its activities in mission, unity, justice and service. Why is its fostering of renewal a comparatively awkward function for the Council?

1. The differing ways in which Christians understand renewal may keep them from seeing it as a priority for the ecumenical movement. Some traditions emphasize the divine origin of the church as a perfect society which cannot be changed or improved; renewal, they insist, can take place only in the lives of individual Christians. Those who believe that renewal will come only with the new heaven and new earth may meanwhile complacently accept the status quo; while others who look to a perfect church on earth may see "renewal" as a process of separating oneself from the sin and imperfection in existing churches.

2. The life of the local Christian community is at the heart of any renewal of the church. Here, at the local level, is where most Christians worship and witness, and where sharing and confessing takes place. To be sure, an indispensable condition for, and consequence of, any real renewal is a breakdown of parochial attitudes. Yet the structure of the WCC allows little direct contact between the Council and local congregations. For one thing, it is practically impossible for a body with headquarters in Geneva to reach into more than a handful of the hundreds of thousands of congregations that belong to its member churches. Even a national church office in a larger country – with which the WCC does indeed relate directly – may have limited influence on its affiliated congregations.

3. Much of the dynamism for renewing the church comes from groups and movements who feel a specific vocation that takes shape outside the institutional structures. House churches and prayer cells meeting in someone's home, charismatic renewal groups, Pentecostal churches with an independent and congregational structure, African Instituted Churches meeting outside, evangelical caucuses within a member church, Christian action groups that campaign for disarmament or the end of apartheid or for a new life-style – these may all, in their different ways, represent creative efforts to live out the faith in a renewed and renewing way.

The WCC prizes its contacts with such groups and movements, recognizing that the work of the Holy Spirit is not limited to institutional bodies that relate to a council of churches. Yet these various groups can remain isolated from the wider ecumenical fellowship, and fail to make their potential contribution to renewal.

4. As Christians pray for the coming of God's kingdom, they quite naturally emphasize different aspects of their obedience to the call of the Spirit. This can lead those active in struggles against injustice to undervalue those who focus on liturgical life, and both to keep away from those who stress conversion and personal holiness. The stronger the convictions that animate their commitment to one of such fields of work, the greater the tension is likely to grow between that group and Christians with other priorities. Each group is tempted to see its own priority as non-negotiable and other emphases as optional. The result is that the overall force for renewal is diminished.

5. Even if the call for renewal of the church is not a call to abandon convictions and traditions, it is an appeal for change. Any call for change, especially from a body such as the WCC, which may seem remote from the realities of any local situation, will meet the inertia of the status quo, if not the outright resistance of those who have a stake in maintaining it.

* * *

Methods of work

With this survey of *what* the WCC does behind us, we can look more briefly at *how* the Council works: some of the typical and most frequent methods by which it carries out the initiatives for unity, witness, service, justice and renewal.

Prayer

"God of unity, God of love, what we say with our lips, make strong in our hearts; what we affirm with our minds, make vivid in our lives. Send us your Spirit to pray in us what we dare not pray, to claim us beyond our own claims, to bind us when we are tempted to go our own ways. Lead us forward. Lead us together. Lead us to do your will, the will of Jesus Christ, our Lord. Amen."

With that prayer, the members of the 1998 WCC assembly in Harare re-committed themselves to "Our Ecumenical Vision" and sent each other out to work for goals that the assembly had set. It stands here to indicate the priority that – from the beginning, indeed from before anyone could have talked about a beginning – has been given to prayer, the characteristic way by which Christians have sought to let their thoughts and plans be over-ruled and reshaped by the living Spirit.

Prayer vigils were held from the earliest days of interchurch gatherings. The oldest manifestation of ecumenical concern for one another is the *Week of Prayer for Christian Unity*, started in 1908 by Father Paul Wattson in the USA, and reinvigorated by Father Paul Couturier in France in 1935 with the inclusive basis that prayer should be "for the unity Christ wills by the means he wills". This Week is observed in the Northern hemisphere chiefly in the eight days between feasts of St Peter and St Paul in January (18-25), and in the South at Pentecost. It is also the most substantial programme carried through jointly between the WCC and the Roman Catholic Church.

The *Ecumenical Prayer Cycle* is another instrument of prayer. In its simplest form this cycle is no more than a list of countries, with their churches, laid out so that they correspond to the 52 weeks of a year. The booklet in which this cycle is published provides brief information, but the existence of the cycle can encourage and inspire groups and churches to seek out other sources and openings for prayer – for instance by inviting someone from the region or country concerned to speak to them that week. So the cycle is both a fruit of ecumenical solidarity and an instrument to root that solidarity more deeply.

Meetings

Virtually any account of the international ecumenical movement or the WCC will be sprinkled with the names of cities followed by dates (Oxford 1938, New Delhi 1961, etc.) marking important conferences or consultations. In fact, the story of any ecumenical meeting begins much earlier – with preparatory soundings and correspondence, draft study papers, even sometimes preliminary contacts – and continues long after the actual meeting, with reports, publications and perhaps details of the new programmes and follow-through efforts that the meeting decided on.

In its early years the WCC was found to be holding some 20 meetings a year, as well as the succession of courses and seminars at the Ecumenical Institute at Bossey. The centrality of such a priority on meetings is of course not without its critics. To bring people from around the world costs much time and money, especially when the costs of translation of documents and simultaneous interpretation are included. For every meeting that achieves the status of an ecumenical landmark, there are many which are soon forgotten. Reports drafted and redrafted long after midnight in order to forge a common statement from the input of all participants may look less impressive a day or two later.

Yet the personal interaction among people at a conference is one of the best ways for the WCC to fulfil its role as a forum for the many gifts and insights within the church

A Bossey graduate school certificate, dated 23 July 1948

Nos vœux et notre affection
vous accompagnent

John Bodo

vous qui avez suivi les cours
et pris une part active
aux séminaires et à la vie

de la Communauté de l'INSTITUT ŒCUMÉNIQUE
lors de sa VIIIe session, du 5 au 23 juillet 1948

Le Directeur Général   Le Directeur   Le Chargé des cours

I Pierre 2 (2-5)   CHATEAU DE BOSSEY, par CÉLIGNY (Suisse)

throughout the world. At conferences the participants can take a direct share in the work of the Council, and then both report on that work and stand part-responsible for it at home.

Some conferences are designed to pursue studies undertaken by the WCC, aiming to discern and articulate convergences between the churches on important and divisive issues. In chapter 5 below we take a closer look at the Council's role in carrying through and stimulating intellectual work.

Visits

Many different sorts of visits contribute to the life and work of the WCC. Conference participants, before and after the meeting, will give time to visiting conferences and committees of their own and other churches in their home areas, in order to prepare for and then report back on the conference. So too the staff of the WCC are constantly on the move, informing people about their specific work as about the more general concerns of the Council, and learning more closely how different issues are seen in different areas. A third form of visit, by an interchurch team, has come to play a key role in exemplifying the work of the WCC. Such a visit is a striking sign of the solidarity that churches in the WCC learn to express with and for one another.

In its broadest sense, ecumenical solidarity is rooted in the vision of "one human family in justice and peace" under the loving care of God. The urgency of realizing this is heightened by growing awareness that many contemporary problems, most obviously those of nuclear weapons and of ecological threats, cannot be overcome without transcending the boundaries of nations and cultures. So a team visit, involving people from three and more "sides" of a significant problem, is a particularly effective way of witnessing.

Such a universal solidarity does not mean never taking sides. Where people are suffering injustice, the readiness of churches around the world to identify with their struggle can be a powerful encouragement. Money channelled to them, or the publication of information about their struggle, can prove to be of important assistance to their cause. But in many cases the most vivid demonstration of solidarity will be a pastoral visit from representatives of other churches in the WCC. Indeed, in the case of those who have long been marginalized into poverty and neglect, signs of solidarity with them from elsewhere become not just an *expression* of faith but something which touches on the very *essence* of faith.

Yet ecumenical solidarity is not one-directional. WCC general secretary Emilio Castro once spoke of the solidarity of churches in Asia, Africa and Latin America with churches in the West whose struggle is quite different – "where it's not oppression but the seductions of a consumer society that need to be confronted: where the challenge is to recover faith within a secular society that has no place for God... In that situation, the solidarity of those struggling elsewhere can bring a vivacity and joy to faith and a challenge and invitation to young people."

Channelling resources

Many Christians have caught the vision of one Christian family throughout the world through the receiving or sending of personnel and funds for mission, interchurch aid and development. Although the WCC no longer operates or staffs local mission or service programmes, it has served as a channel for substantial amounts of money and material aid sent from churches, their agencies, other humanitarian organizations or governments. Sometimes this has fostered the misconception that the WCC is nothing but a funding agency, to the exclusion of its other functions.

Yet there are still deeper problems arising from the large overseas programmes of some wealthy churches in the North, sending large amounts of money and people to certain churches in the South. Within the WCC, efforts have been devoted to overcoming the idea that a church is *either* a sending *or* a receiving body, and to breaking down the mental structures of inequality or dependency this inevitably creates.

The name given to this emphasis is Ecumenical Sharing of Resources (ESR). It is rooted in the understanding that churches have spiritual, cultural and human resources as well as material or financial ones. ESR calls for just relationships based on interdependence – equality, mutual accountability and the sharing of power. It requires holding together mission and service, which are often treated separately, both in theology and in the organizational structures of many churches.

To translate these insights and ideals into reality has however proved difficult, for the churches and for the WCC. In 1980 the WCC central committee sent a message about ESR to the churches. In 1987 it called a world consultation at El Escorial in Spain, under the theme: "Koinonia – Sharing Life in a World Community". The consultation adopted a set of "Guidelines for Sharing", and formulated a "Common Discipline of Ecumenical Sharing".

Theologically, ESR grows out of the understanding of each local church as a sharing community, rooted in the eucharist, from which it is sent out again and again to be Christ's body, broken and shared in and for the life of the world. The global fellowship of churches is called no less to reflect that same image of the body. Thus the search for the real meaning of the one eucharist and for recovering the proper unity of the body broken there for the life of the world is bound up with the task of building the ecumenical community of sharing.

Public issues

Already in its founding assembly in 1948 the WCC acknowledged a "clear obligation to speak out" on some "vital issues". Ever since, many voices keep calling for "the church" to speak publicly on current issues of concern. Yet reservations about such statements have an equally long history: Amsterdam added that "it is certainly undesirable that the Council should issue such pronouncements often".

WCC rules specify *how* the Council may speak publicly, *who* may speak for it, *when* it is appropriate to speak, and *what authority* such statements will have – no more than "the weight which they carry by their own truth and wisdom". Fundamental to all this is the reason *why* the WCC is involved in "political matters". One answer is to be found in the *Ecumenical Affirmation on Mission and Evangelism* of 1982 (see p. 40 above): "The biblical promise of a new earth and a new heaven where love, peace and justice will prevail invites our action as Christians in history." To be non-political, to say and do nothing, is to give tacit support to the way things are.

Not that the ecumenical movement has any blueprint for global policy. Concepts such as "the Responsible Society" in the 1950s, a "Just, Participatory and Sustainable Society" in the 1970s, or "Justice, Peace and the Integrity of Creation" after the 1983 Vancouver assembly have offered trenchant critique of the status quo and have pointed to the imperative of breaking out of its straitjacket. But they have not attempted to put forward any specific plan for how life on earth should be ordered.

Elements of the biblical vision of the kingdom of God – a reign of wholeness and harmony, of peace, justice and righteousness, of healing and salvation, of freedom, prosperity and well-being – present an abiding judgment on the way things are in this world. When churches speak and act together on world issues, they are seeking to bear witness to the good news, to combine the hope and promise of the vision of God's kingdom with a call to repentance that is both accurate and convincing in its grasp of current political, social and economic realities.

Behind any WCC action on public issues is its constant work of monitoring, analyzing and interpreting political developments and conflicts in the world, and of identifying how these affect the life and witness of the churches. Information is collected and interpreted from a variety of sources, especially churches, and may suggest various types of action: a delegation to visit a church in a critical situation, representations to officials of one or more governments, either directly or through churches or United Nations, diplomatic or non-governmental channels. In search of channels for the peaceful resolution of conflicts, the WCC may provide a means of communication between the parties, explore the resources of the churches in neighbouring areas or offer itself to help with negotiations.

What sorts of situations warrant public statements in addition to such action? The central committee has identified some criteria: situations in which the WCC has "direct involvement and long-standing commitment" (e.g. the status of Jerusalem); emerging issues calling for action by the churches (e.g. the unrepayable debts of many countries in the South); critical and developing political situations in which publicizing the WCC's judgment would be helpful (e.g. child soldiers); situations about which member churches expect the WCC to speak out (e.g. globalization); and situations in which a public statement can set policies for WCC staff (e.g. the 1998 Harare assembly's statement on human rights).

One must always be cautious about claiming that any WCC statement has directly influenced the course of affairs. Political decision-making is complex, and few governments gladly admit that they are influenced by outside pressure. Nonetheless public opinion undoubtedly carries some weight, and the WCC may add to that or help to mobilize it. Its special knowledge or moral standing may add credibility to a campaign.

However, there may also be a negative impact. A statement can create difficulties for one or more member churches. Although the Council seeks to consult with member churches in every situation about which it is preparing a statement, the global perspective may suggest a response contrary to the advice of those churches. The Council's political analysis or judgment may be questioned. Most often, however, it is not so much individual statements that are criticized as what the critic considers the bias in the selection of issues chosen for public comment.

Communication

Telling the stories of the WCC to the member churches and the general public is complicated by the variety of topics the Council covers, the sensitive, sometimes controversial nature of some of the stands it takes, and the diversity of those with whom it seeks to communicate. The most effective communication takes place face-to-face, between Christians from different churches when they can have time together, or on occasions when WCC staff and others familiar with the Council can engage in direct conversation with those eager to know more. Yet such occasions are inevitably limited; most of the time enquirers have to be content with reading.

Many programmes within the WCC keep in regular contact with their particular networks by means of newsletters – whether those concerned with race relations, with professional issues in health care, with theological education.

Providing news and interpretation of the life and work of the WCC as a whole, encouraging information-sharing between the churches and helping the WCC to get its witness known through the world's press and broadcasting,

Patriarch Alexei of Moscow and All Russia speaking to the media at the summit of the primates of the Orthodox churches, held in Istanbul in March 1992

are tasks of its Office of Communication. This office holds a substantial photographic library, used by many periodicals around the world. News from the churches and the WCC is published regularly through *Ecumenical News International*, a collaborative press service sponsored jointly by the WCC, the Lutheran World Federation, the World Alliance of Reformed Churches and the Conference of European Churches. The WCC also publishes two substantial quarterly journals, *The Ecumenical Review* and the *International Review of Mission*, as well as some 20 books a year.

WCC finances

Giving and receiving, as we have seen, belong to the essence of ecumenical fellowship. While the Council's finances are hardly a "way of working" alongside others, they are one measure of its health and vitality.

The technicalities of finance put some people off. Others prefer not to look too far, in case they become aware of "the one who pays the piper calling the tune", or find that "financial realism" dulls the cutting edge of creative engagement. Moreover, WCC finances are essentially complex because many aspects are always changing – currency exchange rates, interest rates, contribution levels of member churches, and so on.

In recent years the WCC's annual total budget has provided for expenditures of some 27 million Swiss francs. This amount does not include the grants made by the WCC in the broad range of its project work, or the funds which the WCC channels to activities of member churches and of national or regional councils of churches around the world, of an average total of 23 million Swiss francs per year. The WCC, it should be noted, has not charged for transferring the second category of funds, though their handling involves expense, including banking charges, staff time for reporting and efforts to raise money within this whole programme. Income and expenses for WCC assemblies, held every seven years or so, are also budgeted separately.

The major source of income to cover the Council's expenses is the contributions from its member churches and their specialized agencies. Some of the WCC's programmes are also supported by funds received from governments, other organizations and individual donors. Moreover the WCC receives income from fees paid to the Ecumenical Institute and from the sale of publications, as from rental of office space in the Geneva Ecumenical Centre and from investments. Yet for several years now it has been proving increasingly difficult to raise income sufficient to keep pace with rising expenses. Among the factors which contribute to this are:

- Some member churches who contribute substantially to the WCC have been facing financial problems of their own and have had to cut their contributions. Because of the unbalanced world financial situation, the largest part of the WCC's income comes from West European and North American churches. Many member churches in the South and East give generously in comparison with their resources, but their economic circumstances prevent them from ranking among the major donors.

- Designated income, earmarked for particular programmes, has continued to rise. But the more flexible undesignated contributions, vital for maintaining the WCC's central organization and for supporting programmes which do not attract designated giving, have not kept pace with rising expenditure.

- Staff costs represent some 70 percent of the WCC's expenditure; the staff has been reduced from about 340 in 1990 to 190 in 2001, of whom 73 are programme and technical and 119 administrative staff.

- As an international body, the WCC receives its income in many currencies. With its headquarters in Geneva, it must convert that money into Swiss francs to cover most of its operating expenses. Given the fluctuations of exchange rates, even increased giving to the Council may not mean higher receipts. At the same time, inflation must be taken into account when comparing the value of income over the years.

At the 1998 assembly in Harare, the finance committee reaffirmed the principle that "every member church should meet its membership contribution", and set a target of 10 million Swiss francs for undesignated income from member churches to be met by the year 2005. It further asked the churches to observe one Sunday in the year for focusing on the WCC and for raising money to support it.

4. An Inclusive Community

All very impressive, but just what holds it all together? How does it all relate to the United Nations? Or to the Vatican? What part do local or national councils of churches play? And how do ordinary Christians get involved?

Questions like these prompt a more careful look at both the internal structures by which the WCC pursues its work and the relations it needs to maintain with bodies outside its own immediate community, whether Christian churches that have decided not to apply for membership or other bodies with different purposes.

Moreover, the WCC has in many countries come to enjoy a reputation for controversial actions. Most people, if they stop to think about it at all, would probably approve such WCC actions as responding to an earthquake with immediate help and long-range re-development assistance, or the publication of materials for the Week of Prayer for Christian Unity. That the WCC is busy promoting Christian unity, common witness, worldwide service and effective renewal does not raise anyone's hackles. Yet as soon as a specific change is pressed or advocated in the name of the WCC – for example, the dissolution of apartheid so that South Africa could become a fully multi-racial nation, or the ordination of women to the priesthood so that all God's gifts can be brought to bear in ministry – some people will protest. How can it happen that a council of the churches can do or say something about which my church is not happy? What authority does the WCC claim, and on what grounds?

To answer such questions, this chapter will look first at the internal operations of the Council, then at its authority, and finally at its wider relationships – with churches not in its membership, with representatives of other religious communities, and with other international organizations.

Levels of decision-making

The World Council of Churches has four main levels at which decisions are taken: the assembly, meeting about every seven years, to which every member church is invited to send at least one delegate; the central committee of 150 persons, elected by the assembly from among those delegates, which meets every 12-18 months; the executive committee of up to 25 persons, elected by and from among the central committee, meeting twice a year; and the general secretary and staff teams responsible for carrying through both the actual decisions and the continuing concerns of the Council.

The assembly is the supreme legislative body governing the life and work of the Council. It is made up of delegates, almost 1000, appointed by the member churches. The number of delegates to which each church is entitled is determined by its size (every member church may send at least one delegate), with allowance made in the allocation of delegates for balancing confessional, cultural and geographical representation. In addition to the delegates, a comparable number of people attend as observers, consultants, guests and staff, joined by a listening crowd of journalists and other media people, and by many visitors.

The assembly becomes a mixture of parliament and festival, the shop window where the WCC displays the range of churches and persons who compose it, the scope and nature of the activities it pursues, the goals and quality of its programmes, and virtually everything else about it that can serve as a model for the churches and the world.

Worship and group Bible study enrich the assembly's spiritual and theological life. Other group sessions allow for debate and for discovering friendships across all kinds of boundaries. Visits to local parishes on a Sunday help to anchor the global experience in local realities. Major platform addresses give the assembly food to digest, while work in committees provides key texts and resolutions for the whole assembly to vote on in the final days.

Overall, each assembly is expected to review what the Council has done over the previous seven years and to set guidelines for the years ahead. It cannot be the place for many detailed decisions apart from the election of the presidents and the central committee.

Over the years, the WCC has sought to become increasingly *participatory* in its processes. Selection of delegates, for instance, has become a somewhat complex matter. Originally calculated in relation to the size of each church, these figures have had to make allowance for balancing out the various confessional families, regions of the world and cultural groupings. Moreover, while each church will have its own way of selecting its delegates, they are all urged to do so in ways that will ensure a proper distribution of church officials, local church ministers and lay people, as well as of men, women and younger people (under 30). Still more, the central committee has been given power to improve the balance by picking names out of lists submitted by the churches for up to an additional 15 percent of the delegates.

All the same there can be no perfect way of ensuring "full participation" in ways that will suit everyone. The limited size of the delegation from many member churches makes it impossible for each church to fill all categories. Moreover the need for a cross-section of people often comes into tension with the need for people with experience and expertise. It is easy for either "fuller participation" or "qualified and committed people" to crowd each other out. The WCC, like many other organizations, needs a mix of "collective memory" and "new blood", never easily balanced. And of course representation does not necessarily ensure real *participation*!

The central committee is responsible for implementing the priorities and policies laid down by the assembly. At each of its meetings it reviews the activities of the commissions and staff. It will, as appropriate, adjust priorities and approve new emphases and programmes. It elects the general secretary and other senior staff, and names people – often from nominations sent in by the churches – to serve on standing commissions and ad hoc advisory bodies. While not every church can have a member on the central committee, care is taken to see that the different confessions and continents are all represented, so that lines of reporting back into the life of all churches can be readily devised.

The central committee elects up to 20 of its members to serve as *the executive committee* of the WCC, along with the

The WCC general secretaries

Above: From left to right: Eugene Carson Blake (USA), Philip Potter (West Indies) and W.A. Visser 't Hooft (Netherlands)

Below: Emilio Castro (Uruguay) and Konrad Raiser (Germany)

WCC

central committee officers – moderator, two vice-moderators and the general secretary, as well as the moderators of the programme and finance committees of the central committee. Meeting twice a year, the executive committee's role in policy-making is limited to matters specifically referred to it by the central committee – apart from unforeseen emergencies, in regard to which it may take provisional decisions. It appoints programme staff, monitors ongoing work, and supervises the budget approved by the central committee.

As the chief executive officer of the Council, the *general secretary* is responsible to the central and executive committees for coordinating all WCC activities. At the same time the general secretary plays a key role in relating with and interpreting the Council's work to member churches, national and regional ecumenical bodies, and the wider world. A senior Staff Leadership Group meets weekly, and a larger Staff Consultative Group monthly.

In the more flexible structure which went into effect after the 1997 central committee approved the statement on the "Common Understanding and Vision of the WCC", the staff of 175 full-time posts is expected to function as a "single administrative whole". For practical purposes, it is subdivided into 15 teams working in four major clusters: Issues and Themes; Relations; Communication; and Finance, Services and Administration. The Ecumenical Institute is attached directly to the General Secretariat.

The staff carry through the day-to-day operations in accordance with the policies laid down. The rules specify the "primary need for competence" and for "dedication to the aims and spirit of the WCC" in the persons appointed as staff. The WCC also seeks to recruit staff "on as wide a geographical and confessional basis as possible, and without distinction as to race and sex".

Given that the budget limits the number of staff, not all member churches can expect it to include a person from their ranks. There are other factors which make it difficult to achieve the balance the central committee seeks. Many churches appoint few women to positions that provide them with the experience needed for working in the WCC. Many churches also expect qualities in their senior leaders that rely on talents of less use in an international fellowship. The WCC also has to rely on a command of English in virtually all its staff, which cuts out many excellent people. At the same time many churches, especially the smaller, are reluctant to "lose" a good leader to the international ecumenical movement whom it will be very difficult to replace "at home". Nonetheless, the WCC staff team is a lively and significant community, whose members can be expected, on returning home, to contribute greatly to their own churches in later years.

Related interchurch organizations

While strictly speaking outside the WCC, three groups of organizations formed by churches play a part in the life – and to some extent in the decision-making – of the ecumenical movement as a whole. Some are organized geographically (national Christian councils and regional ecumenical organizations), others are international groupings of churches within a single confessional tradition (Lutheran World Federation, Baptist World Alliance, etc.), others again are world ecumenical organizations focusing on a specific task or issue (e.g. the United Bible Societies), or a specific constituency (e.g. the World Student Christian Federation and the YM/YWCA).

Regional and national interchurch bodies. The churches have established *regional* interchurch bodies in Africa, Asia, the Caribbean, Europe, Latin America, the Middle East and the Pacific. (No such regional body exists in North America.)

Besides inviting these "essential partners in the ecumenical enterprise" to be represented in their own right (yet without vote) at meetings of WCC governing bodies, the World Council is regularly in contact with them on ecumenical developments in their areas.

National councils of churches (NCCs) have been formed in some 90 countries. Some relate to the WCC as "associated councils", entitled to non-voting representation at assemblies and meetings of the central committee. Others are "affliated" with the WCC's Commission on World Mission and Evangelism but prefer not to be directly associated with the WCC as a whole. A third category is formed by Christian councils "in working relationship" with the WCC – often functioning as channels of communication and cooperation with the WCC in areas of interchurch aid, refugee and world service.

These national councils are diverse in the number of their member churches, of their staff, and in the size of their budgets. Their origins vary greatly too, though the majority can be traced back to the worldwide missionary movement in the early part of the 20th century. How they see their role and authority also varies widely. Many of them are linked with a network of *local* councils, carrying out comparable tasks.

As with the WCC, most of these regional, national and local bodies are formed by churches. Many churches find it natural to belong to ecumenical bodies at the local, national, regional and world levels. Yet the relationships between these levels are *not* structured hierarchically; organizations for smaller geographical areas are *not* subsumed under those for larger; the WCC is *not* the "supreme" body at the top of the ladder. Each such local, national or regional body is itself a fellowship of churches, with its own autonomy, not a branch office of the WCC.

An important contribution made by many of these national and regional bodies comes from the participation in them, by full or associate membership, of the Roman Catholic Church. Its decision for membership in each case is made by the relevant national or regional conference of Catholic bishops, and the Vatican has spoken positively of NCCs as one of the more important forms of ecumenical cooperation.

Christian world communions. In a strict interpretation of the term, these organizations are not directly "ecumenical", since their member churches come from a single confessional tradition. Yet many of them participate in theological dialogues across confessional lines. At the same time the situations of their member churches often lead these world bodies to share many of the concerns on the WCC's agenda. In certain instances they provide an entry point into the ecumenical fellowship for churches that have had no contact with the WCC.

Shared concerns may produce overlapping, even competitive programmes. A particular sore spot has often been the sending of assistance for development programmes "bi-laterally", along confessional lines, rather than through the WCC. Yet the formation of Action of Churches Together (see above, p. 67) has helped to overcome this, at least with regard to assistance in situations of emergencies.

Specialized ecumenical bodies. There are a considerable number of such bodies, with which the WCC has more or less regular and structured relationships. The WCC largely grew out of the YMCA, YWCA and World Student Christian Federation (see above, pp. 21ff.), and maintains relationships with them. The WCC also collaborates with bodies such as the United Bible Societies, the World Association for Christian Communication, and the International Fellowship of Reconciliation. At present, the WCC recognizes some twenty "international ecumenical organizations" with which it maintains working relationships. And it is open to cooperation with others.

The question of authority

Setting out the Council's pattern of decision-making and internal relationships answers only part of the question of its authority. It must also always be asked: Just what *weight* can the WCC claim for what it says and does?

Authority was a major point of debate in the early negotiations that led to the integration of the various streams of united Christian endeavour into a world council of churches. For the different churches and traditions have widely different notions of their own authority.

Two passages in the WCC's Constitution and Rules address these questions. Article IV of the Constitution lays down the overall policy:

> The World Council shall offer counsel and provide opportunity for united action in matters of common interest.
>
> It may take action on behalf of constituent churches only in such matters as one or more of them may commit to it and only on behalf of such churches.
>
> The World Council shall not legislate for the churches; nor shall it act for them in any manner except as indicated above or as may hereafter be specified by the constituent churches.

Article X of the Rules then describes the authority of WCC public statements:

> While such statements may have great significance and influence as the expressions of the judgment or concern of so widely representative a Christian body, yet their authority will consist only in the weight which they carry by their own truth and wis-

dom, and the publishing of such statements shall not be held to imply that the World Council as such has, or can have, any constitutional authority over the constituent churches or right to speak for them.

These two articles can be read as putting the accent on how the WCC's authority is limited: the Council may not make rules for the churches, speak for them, act for them (except when they specifically ask it to) or indeed give the impression that it exercises any kind of authority over them. It is a *council* of churches, yet not in the authoritative sense of those gatherings of the early church when bishops took decisions binding the whole church.

In the tradition of some churches, this limitation of the WCC's authority will seems so obvious, so in line with their own internal patterns, as scarcely to warrant mentioning. The idea that the WCC does not exercise authority over its member churches will strike many Christians as a consequence of the belief that *no* church body can bind the conscience of its individual members. Indeed, some churches have stayed out of the WCC precisely because it claims no authority to ensure that *all* its member churches will in fact adhere to the theological affirmations in the WCC Basis!

But to emphasize only this negative side is to overlook a more dynamic understanding which reflects the Council's heritage as a *movement* towards Christian unity. To be sure, the WCC cannot claim canonical authority for what it says and does, but it *is* mandated to "offer counsel" to the churches, and to enable them to take "united action". There is an expectation that, in reflecting the considered judgment or concern of a wide group of Christians, what the WCC says will not only express "truth and wisdom" but also have "significance and influence".

This more dynamic understanding of the WCC's significance and influence presupposes several convictions on the part of its member churches. When these are present, the WCC can – and indeed does – exercise a kind of authority – not, to be sure, an authority *over* the churches, but an authority *through* them.

• By joining the World Council, a church acknowledges that the unity Christ wants for his followers is not presently manifest. It expresses what the WCC's 1950 "Toronto Statement", on "The Church, the Churches, and the World Council of Churches", called "a holy dissatisfaction" with the status quo. In that sense, a WCC member church is entitled to hope that its participation in the Council's life will change the status quo.

• All the churches in the WCC recognize that "Christ is the Divine Head of the Body", as the Toronto Statement puts it, and that those who acknowledge this are obliged "to enter into real and close relationship with each other". Moreover, they agree that the church of Jesus Christ is more inclusive than the membership of their own church, thus giving each church "a positive task to seek fellowship" with those beyond their own church who also confess the lordship of Christ. "The ecumenical movement is the place where this search and discovery take place."

This primacy of the headship of Christ puts the question of the authority of churches and of the WCC into perspective. That the churches are bound together in fellowship because they are each and all primarily bound to God in Jesus Christ speaks of a unity compelling each of them to reach out and listen to each other before asking questions about authority.

• In order to be true to its name as a *world* fellowship, the WCC seeks to be a forum in which an ever-widening and deepening range of traditions, convictions and experiences is heard. Ideally, its actions and statements will be the stronger the more they echo the diversity of thought and experience among all those who confess the lordship of Christ.

• A church that is serious about its ecumenical commitment will not only listen to these new and wider perspectives, but be ready to learn from them. This implies acknowledging that one's own tradition has something to learn from the encounter with Christians of other backgrounds. There is of course no obligation on any Christian or church to accept whatever is said by some other church or the WCC. But by

joining the WCC, a church signals a self-imposed obligation
to consider that possibility.

• The absence of a binding character in the WCC's words
and deeds does not mean that they are, as it were, projected
into a vacuum. What the WCC says and does receives its val-
idation by a process of *reception* in the member churches.
This process may continue long after the WCC's original
words or actions have receded into history.

In the early days there was perhaps a tendency to suppose that this process could be short-cut by ensuring that (as
Joseph Oldham once wrote) "there are present leading representatives of the churches, who in giving their approval
have reasonable confidence that if the action in question is
challenged in their respective church assemblies they can
successfully defend it". But the passing of time has made
it clear that the process of churches making the words and
actions of the WCC their own is more complicated than
that.

• In the same memorandum Oldham alluded to another
type of authority the actions and statements of the WCC may
take on. This is the authority that comes "because the Holy
Spirit might, to an unlimited extent, speak and exercise influence" through them.

It is wrong to claim this sort of authority ahead of time,
and risky to identify it even in retrospect. Yet there is a spiritual dimension which is fundamental to the ecumenical
enterprise. The still-divided churches cannot always offer a
common witness to the world, the Toronto Statement con-
cedes, "but when it proves possible thus to speak or act
together, the churches can gratefully accept it as God's gra-
cious gift".

• Expressed in human terms, what all this suggests is that
there must be a fundamental relationship of trust characteriz-
ing the fellowship of churches in the WCC.

As we look in the remainder of this chapter at some of the
WCC's relationships, we will see that building and broaden-
ing this trust is not limited to member churches. If what the
WCC says and does is to have "significance and influence",

its relationships with bodies which do not or cannot choose to be part of its fellowship are also important.

Relationships with the member churches

Displaying a marvellous diversity of gifts, living in a wide range of circumstances, worshipping God in a rich profusion of liturgies and languages, the member churches are the building blocks of the WCC. Their members serve on its decision-making and advisory bodies, and constitute the great majority of the programme staff. Their financial contributions provide most of the Council's regular, unearmarked income.

Yet while the Council's relationships with its member churches are fundamental, they are not automatic. Since WCC rules do not specify any mandatory token of a church's participation, a church can continue to be a member without sending representatives to WCC meetings or responding to requests for information or funds. Four factors help to explain why it is often difficult for the WCC to maintain close ties with the member churches.

Worship in the Tagabe congregation of the Church of the Province of Melanesia, on the outskirts of Port-Vila, Vanuatu

• The WCC is inevitably *distant* from its member churches. Most obviously, this distance can be geographical: the WCC offices in Geneva or the site of a major WCC meeting may be too far away for some member churches to have any first-hand contact. The WCC may also be linguistically remote: the records of what it does are almost entirely in European languages – mostly English – and the language of its documents is often technical and difficult for lay people to understand. There may also be a wide cultural gap between styles of procedure in the WCC and those of some member churches.

• The *complexity* of the WCC may discourage churches from developing closer relations with the Council. Church leaders with full portfolios may be overwhelmed – or annoyed – by the quantity and variety of WCC activities they are asked to support. Misunderstandings and misconceptions may arise. The result may be that within a given church the WCC will have no more than a few enthusiastic advocates.

• The ecumenical ideal that "the churches should act together in all matters except those in which deep differences of conviction compel them to act separately" is still far from being realized. Even for those things which churches *do* undertake together, the WCC is only one among a variety of instruments. Consequently, relations between the WCC and its member churches may be strained by the appearance of *competition* with a church's own programmes or with those it undertakes in other forms of interchurch cooperation.

• No matter how carefully the decision-making process within the WCC takes into account the different points of view among its constituency, *disagreement* may arise between a member church – or a substantial part of one – and the WCC.

Visits to member churches by WCC staff and officers are perhaps the most effective way to strengthen the Council's ties with them. But since the size of the WCC staff is not large, in comparison with the number of member churches, such visits are usually made in connection with specific programmes.

Two groups of member churches deserve special mention.

United and uniting churches

These are national or regional churches formed by the union of two or more denominations from the same or different confessional traditions. Most are the result of the 20th-century ecumenical movement, though the first united church was formed from Lutheran and Reformed churches in Prussia in 1817. The first major union of the 20th century was the United Church of Canada in 1925; most others have been formed since the second world war in formerly colonized nations of the South, especially in the late 1960s and early 1970s. They see themselves as having a distinctive experience and contribution to make within a council serving Christian unity. So it is in them that the vision underlying the entire ecumenical movement receives its most concrete test.

As was laid down in the 1950 Toronto Statement, the WCC is not an agency "to negotiate unions between churches, which can only be done by the churches themselves, acting on their own initiative". If invited, however, the WCC will send observers to advise on church union negotiations. The Faith and Order commission has sponsored five worldwide consultations of representatives of these churches, and publishes every second year a survey of ongoing union negotiations between churches.

The cost of organic union was highlighted by the WCC's third assembly (New Delhi 1961), when it noted that "the achievement of unity will involve nothing less than a death and rebirth of many forms of church life as we have known them". Indeed, some church leaders have argued that the effort required to overcome confessional division (especially to reconcile different forms of ordained ministry and to ease fears of "loss of identity") is misplaced. There are, they say, more important challenges to the church. Since the 1970s the rise of globally organized theological dialogues between different confessions seems to have diverted much attention away from church union negotiations at the national level.

Recent church union conversations have thus put more emphasis on the need to achieve union by stages, and on exploring forms of union which can allow churches to enter into full communion while retaining something of their specific historic identities.

In addition to the sort of "cost of union" identified by New Delhi, uniting churches may have to pay in more concrete ways. Sometimes they find themselves losing financial support from European or North American churches of the denominational heritage they are giving up for the sake of the union. When a union crosses confessional lines, they may no longer feel at home in a world confessional body (Lutheran, Methodist, Anglican, etc.) though the united and uniting churches have consistently resisted the formation of a "confessional family" of their own. Even within the structures of the WCC there may be a sense in which they feel penalized, since the number of representatives at an assembly to which a united church is entitled will generally be fewer than the total of its parent bodies.

Nonetheless, the WCC remains committed to encouraging all churches along the way to the full overcoming of the splits and divisions of earlier centuries.

Orthodox churches

The first church to publish an appeal to form something like a World Council of Churches was the Ecumenical Patriarchate of Constantinople. In an encyclical letter "Unto the Churches of Christ Everywhere" in 1920, it suggested a body in analogy to the League of Nations. So even if the ecumenical movement is often considered a Protestant initiative – and the majority of church divisions have occurred within the Protestant world – the Orthodox churches have played a central part in the WCC.

Although Orthodox leaders were active in the meetings leading to the formation of the WCC in 1948, not all the Orthodox churches joined at the beginning. Just a month before the Amsterdam assembly, a meeting of Orthodox leaders in Moscow discouraged participation in the WCC.

Despite that recommendation (largely based on a misunderstanding of what the WCC aimed at) some forty Orthodox delegates attended the first assembly.

In the years after 1948 the WCC maintained contacts with all the Orthodox churches. The 1950 Toronto Statement allayed fears of a "super-church" that some Orthodox had felt. Ecumenical relief and development aid attested to the tangible values of solidarity within the WCC. Slowly the obstacles were overcome; and at the third assembly (1961) or soon after, all the remaining Orthodox churches were welcomed into membership.

The Orthodox presence in the WCC has been mutually enriching, but relations have by no means always been smooth. To understand the role of the Orthodox churches in the WCC requires the recognition of their distinctive historical experience as well as of their theological convictions.

The 1920 encyclical of the Patriarchate of Constantinople was a response to its emergence from centuries of isolation, suffering, persecution and martyrdom under the newly defeated Ottoman empire. From 1917 on, some Orthodox churches have endured the difficulties of life under Marxist governments committed to atheism and unwilling to allow the church any public role except that of worship – and often making even that very difficult. Others have long experience of living as minority churches in predominantly Muslim countries. Still others, especially in North and South America and Australia, have had to cope with the challenges of life as being immigrant churches in diaspora.

Fundamental to the Orthodox participation in the ecumenical movement is the belief that unity in faith is an absolute condition for the reunion of divided churches. Church unity must be unity in the apostolic truth, and not just in an external structure for common action. "Ecumenism of space", i.e. Christian unity in every part of the world, cannot be separated from "ecumenism in time", i.e. faithfulness to the apostolic and patristic teaching of the early church. So Orthodox see their vocation within the fellowship of the

WCC as that of holding up the universality and continuity of the one and holy Tradition.

In line with this, Orthodox participants at major conferences, even before the founding of the WCC, have often issued separate statements on important issues, highlighting their divergences from the majority Protestant views. In

A wedding party outside an Armenian Apostolic Church in Yerevan

recent years they have often held preliminary consultations before WCC assemblies so as to feed their approach into the preparations for the meeting.

It is in theology and liturgy that the presence of the Orthodox churches has been most influential in the WCC. Renewed appreciation of the trinitarian character of Christian theology, which many say enriched the christocentric tones of the early years of the WCC, owes much to the Orthodox. So also, as ecumenical worship has evolved, the Orthodox influence has often been felt. As ecological concern has awakened ecumenical interest in the theology of creation, Orthodox theology has provided rich resources. And the model of unity as "a conciliar fellowship of local churches which are themselves truly united" – articulated by the WCC's fifth assembly in Nariobi in 1975 – mirrors in many ways the relationship of the independent and self-governing local (i.e. national) Orthodox churches, themselves united in conciliar fellowship.

Orthodox leaders acknowledge that they have also gained considerably from participation in the ecumenical movement. In some cases it has been practical assistance – aid to refugees or victims of natural disaster, support to help restore monasteries or build theological institutes, opportunities to send their members abroad for training or to participate in ecumenical meetings. The WCC has also been an instrument for introducing other Christians to the often-unknown world of Orthodoxy.

Membership in the WCC has had consequences for internal Orthodox relations, especially the building of contacts between the churches in communion with Constantinople (Eastern Orthodox) and those not part of that communion since the council of Chalcedon in 451 (Oriental Orthodox). Still more, and particularly in connection with the changes in the 1990s in the Soviet Union and other Marxist countries of East and Central Europe, Orthodox leaders have witnessed to the value of what they have learned in the WCC about the role of the church in society – a role many of them were unable to play for many years.

And yet tensions remain. Orthodox participants at the seventh assembly in Canberra (1991) shared several of their concerns in a widely distributed open letter; later that year representatives of both Orthodox families met in Chambésy, near Geneva, for an in-depth discussion of the issues it had raised. The tension was, if anything, stronger and more openly expressed in the eighth assembly (1998), when the decision was taken to establish a special commission, to bring together at least one representative of each Orthodox member church and a similar number of people from other churches, to meet over three years and examine the issues raised by the Orthodox.

A consistent concern for all Orthodox has been their under-representation in WCC assemblies and on the staff. They also fear that, since all the Orthodox churches are now members, Orthodox influence can only wane as more and more new Protestant churches are added. More generally, they are unconvinced that the WCC's style of reaching agreed theological statements really makes it possible for the Orthodox perspective to come through, or that the way the WCC is organized allows enough attention to the priorities of their churches.

In the context of a commitment to "improved Orthodox participation in the ecumenical movement", a document from the Chambésy consultation pointed to other constant worries. It warned against undertaking interfaith dialogue in such a way that "Christian churches acting through WCC agencies should be compromised in their central Christian commitments". It noted that "the Orthodox have had to react against a tendency within the WCC towards a one-sided 'horizontalism'" in social involvements, divorced from the gospel of Jesus Christ. It explained that the Orthodox may not, in conscience, extend or respond to invitations involving "eucharistic hospitality". The continuing division of Christians around the table of the Lord is as painful for them as for any other Christians, but – they insist – eucharistic communion is the supreme expression of the *given unity* of the church and not a means towards *restoring* Christian unity.

Two other subjects of tension should be mentioned. One was noted already in the 1920 encyclical: attempts by Western Christians in traditionally Orthodox countries to win new members for their Protestant churches. WCC statements have repeatedly reaffirmed opposition to proselytism, but the issue continues to surface – even though today most of the Western groups accused of doing this are not affiliated with the WCC or any other ecumenical organization.

The second issue is that of the ordination of women. Orthodox insist that the exclusively male sacramental priesthood in their churches is rooted in the Tradition and does not imply that women are inferior. They agree on the need to discover wider roles for women in the service and spiritual work of the church, including – some have said – the renewal of the institution of deaconesses.

The theological understanding that underlies these views is not shared by most Protestant churches, including some which do not themselves ordain women. Some Protestant churches have in fact moved still further, towards suggesting that the opening of all church offices to both women and men is a core issue of the Christian faith.

A related tension arises over attempts in various churches to make the language used in worship "inclusive" of all people, for instance by replacing the traditional trinitarian formula "Father, Son and Holy Spirit" with names for God that are not directly masculine in gender or attributes, such as "Creator, Redeemer, Sustainer". While most Orthodox would not object in general to the use of different names for God, their churches insist that the traditional formula must be retained in the liturgy.

Relationships with churches not in WCC membership

The Roman Catholic Church

"Why isn't the Roman Catholic Church a member of the World Council of Churches?" is one of the most frequent questions asked about the WCC. One answer is that the Roman Catholic Church has never applied to become a member. In the light of the hopes aroused by the Second Vatican Council in the 1960s, the Vatican and the WCC established a joint study committee to examine the question. But though its report found no insuperable obstacle in theology or canon law, Roman Catholic authorities did not pursue the possibility.

An application from the Roman Catholic Church for membership in the WCC would present practical problems. The size of their church would make questions about balanced representation in WCC governing bodies even more difficult. Moreover, most WCC member churches are self-governing, usually at the national level. The Roman Catholic Church, by contrast, is a worldwide body with a central authority that has universal jurisdiction.

Cardinal Edward Cassidy, former president of the Pontifical Council on Christian Unity, said on several occasions that he did not expect a Roman Catholic application for WCC membership "in the near future", despite the generally good relations between the Council and his church. Indeed these relationships mark a degree of ecumenical advance that would astonish those who remember the hostility of the Vatican authorities to the WCC in its early stages.

Despite overtures from the Faith and Order and Life and Work movements in the 1920s and 1930s, Rome not only stayed outside but declared (in the encyclical *Mortalium Animos* of 1928) that unity could be found only through "the return to the one true church of Christ of all who are separated from it". The ten Catholics who were invited by the WCC as observers to the first assembly in 1948 were forbidden to attend by the Vatican. Similarly the archbishop of Chicago forbade Catholics to attend the second assembly in 1954.

But already by that time new winds were beginning to blow. Informal contacts between WCC and Vatican officials provided useful clarifications, as did more or less secret meetings of theologians of the divided churches. Vatican observers attended the third assembly in 1961. Less than a year later there arrived the crucial turning point in Pope John XXIII's convening of the Second Vatican Council.

Pope John Paul II with general secretary Philip Potter, on the occasion of the pope's visit to the Ecumenical Centre in 1984   WCC

Vatican II's "Decree on Ecumenism" (1964) was the charter for a new openness of the Roman Catholic Church to other churches. It now recognized that "all those justified by faith through baptism are incorporated into Christ" and therefore "have a right to be honoured by the title of Christian, and are properly regarded as brothers in the Lord by the sons of the Catholic church". The Decree calls on Catholics to "esteem the truly Christian endowments from our common heritage... among our separated brethren", for "whatever is truly Christian ... can always result in a more ample realization of the very mystery of Christ and of the church".

A consequence of this shift in attitude has been the encouragement of "common witness" between Catholics and other Christians – through joint celebration of Christian festivals and of the annual Week of Prayer for Christian Unity (international materials for which have for over thirty years been prepared jointly by the WCC and the Roman Catholic Church), through joint approaches to civil authorities about human rights and other social questions.

The highest-level continuing contact between the WCC and the Roman Catholic Church is the Joint Working Group, first established in 1965, which has met every year since and has reported regularly to both parent bodies. It assesses the overall ecumenical situation and discusses such topics as ecumenical formation (the efforts to increase awareness in all churches of the importance of the ecumenical movement), theological and ethical issues related to Christian unity, mixed marriages, and common action on social and political issues.

Beside these contacts, teams within the WCC have working relationships with corresponding agencies within the Roman Catholic Church. Roman Catholic consultants have served on the WCC staff. The Vatican nominates Catholics to places on the WCC Faith and Order commission. Collaboration is well advanced also in the areas of mission and evangelism, interfaith dialogue, health care, diaconal and refugee service, human rights and education.

Moreover, Roman Catholics are active in several international ecumenical bodies in which WCC member churches are also involved. And, as noted above, the growing presence of Roman Catholic representatives in local, national and regional councils of churches helps improve relationships at every level.

Yet obstacles still remain. In some countries where Roman Catholics form the overwhelming majority of the population, other churches may have a much less optimistic assessment of the ecumenical situation. Theological differences still divide Catholics from the members of most WCC member churches, the most familiar of these being the place of the Virgin Mary and the role of the pope. In both these cases what is at one level a problem for ecumenical relationships is at another a matter of debate within the Roman Catholic Church about how it understands itself and the authority of its teachings.

As the experience of over thirty years now shows, working together *de facto* does not resolve the theological question of recognizing each other *de jure*. This lack of official mutual recognition is most evident at the table of the Lord – though this is not strictly a problem between the WCC and the Roman Catholic Church, since by no means all member churches of the Council open their communion table to members of all other WCC churches.

Impediments to unity also arise from different ways of addressing social and ethical issues. Beyond disagreements on questions ranging from abortion and birth control to euthanasia and nuclear deterrence (on all of which there are of course a range of views, often sharply divergent, among WCC member churches), there are significant differences in how to approach ethical questions, and in the authority of church pronouncements on them.

In international relations, the WCC's standing as a non-governmental organization is quite different from that of the Holy See, which has permanent observer status at the United Nations and diplomatic ties with many governments. This difference makes it difficult for the WCC and the RC Church to act jointly on international affairs, even when their positions correspond. The WCC's established policy and process for making public statements on current issues (see above, pp. 98-101) is quite different to the Vatican's.

Evangelicals and Pentecostals

Another important sector of Christians not in the membership of the World Council of Churches, yet with whom the WCC is concerned to cultivate relationships, is referred to in the large terms "evangelical" and "pentecostal".

As used in English, the word "evangelical" commonly refers to Christians who emphasize the authority of the Bible,

A Pentecostal church assembly in Chile   WCC

the individual experience of personal conversion, the calling
to a personal life of growth in holiness, and a passion for the
evangelization of the whole world by calling individuals to
saving faith in Jesus Christ. The word is most straightfor-
wardly used of individual believers and of the independent
groups and agencies such believers often form. It is more difficult to use it as a title for a category of churches, in that in
other languages – not least German – the corresponding word
is synonomous with "Protestant" in English; more than a
quarter of the WCC member churches have the word in their
title when put into English.

Historically it has been in the area of world mission and
evangelism that the WCC and evangelical organizations have
had common interests and significant controversies. Evan-
gelicals have often charged the ecumenical movement with
betraying the true teaching of the Bible, giving too much
attention to social questions and too little to evangelism. Dialogue with people of other living faiths, as discussed and
practised in WCC member churches, has been regarded in
some evangelical quarters as dulling the cutting edge of
evangelism.

Since the 1974 Congress on World Evangelization,
called by the US evangelist Billy Graham in the Swiss city
of Lausanne, there has been considerable contact between
leaders of such groups and the WCC. The chief drafter of
that congress's Covenant, John Stott, spoke a year later at
the Nairobi assembly of the WCC. He urged the Council's

members and the Lausanne constituency to take more note of each other's complementary emphases. Since then there has been a global "evangelical" mission conference held within a month or two of each of the WCC world mission and evangelism conferences. A number of people from each have also attended the other, though it remains clear that a large proportion of those attending each would consider the gulf between them too wide to be bridged by holding a single conference.

Another continuing source of tension within the WCC constituency is the way some wealthy and independent evangelical mission, relief and development agencies, headquartered in North America or Western Europe, operate in countries of the South. Local churches there, some with a long history of struggle as a Christian minority, sometimes charge that the evangelical agencies from the rich North show little respect for the culture and traditions of the area and that, despite their repeated declarations against "the church getting mixed up in politics", they in fact themselves depend on and support a particular thrust of political and economic power.

Yet, many evangelical Christians and groups have a long heritage of costly and thoughtful engagement in society, and serious discussion of social and international justice has been actively pursued in many evangelical circles in recent years.

A different sort of problem arises from the fact that many evangelical groups are not organized as churches. This makes it impossible for them to think about applying to the WCC for formal membership. Unofficial and informal contacts are therefore the best way for mutual relationships to develop.

The 1998 Harare assembly encouraged the central committee to experiment with a new sort of "forum", in which leaders of non-member churches or other Christian groups could be invited to participate.

Pentecostal and independent churches
It is hoped that these forums will include among their participants, alongside people from the Roman Catholic Church,

the evangelical constituencies and the WCC member churches, leaders from what may be the most rapidly growing sector of Christian churches at the beginning of the 21st century, the Pentecostals.

Some features of their spirituality and organization are shared by the no less rapidly growing constituency known as African Instituted Churches which have mushroomed across many parts of Africa. Although they have become a significant part of the worldwide family of Christians, it is difficult to see how they can fit into the structures and expectations of a world body like the WCC.

So, after many earlier contacts, both the Canberra assembly in 1991 and the Harare assembly in 1998 appealed for the broadening and deepening of such encounters. Most congregations of these AICs share a sense of the value of the congregation as a cell in the body of Christ, as a charismatic, healing community, and a vivid belief in a spiritual world in which God's power confronts and overcomes the powers of darkness. The rootedness of these Christians and churches in their own cultures enables them to contextualise the Christian faith and life in ways that missionaries from outside have seldom managed.

The WCC hopes the new forums can discover patterns of contact and collaboration by which these churches can make their full contribution to the total ecumenical movement. Some have felt snubbed by the failure of the missionary churches to take them seriously and to seek their partnership in local and national councils – or by what happened when they offered to join such councils! It has been all too easy for those in leadership of historic denominations to call in question in the Pentecostal and Independent churches a lack of theological depth and training, an authoritarian, charismatic style of leadership, accountable to no wider community, inadequate recognition of the social causes of the poverty of many of their members, an orientation to the life-to-come as an escape from the miseries of the present, excesses of ecstatic enthusiasm. Yet many of these churches are evolving and growing in commitment to social involvement.

Relations with people of other faith traditions

Rooted in the missionary movement, the ecumenical agenda has from the beginning included the question of the relation of Christians to persons of other faiths. Already in planning for the 1910 Edinburgh world missionary conference, a questionnaire on this topic was circulated among missionaries and elicited 157 substantive responses. The great majority of these, the conference's report recalls, stressed the need for "a generous recognition of all that is good and true" in the other religious traditions and communities, as well as for a "universal and emphatic witness to the absoluteness of the Christian faith".

Ninety and more years of discussion within the ecumenical movement have not fully resolved that tension. But the WCC has continued to emphasize the importance of pursuing not just these questions among Christians, but actual relationships. The plurality of religions in so many parts of the world has been given increased urgency by the horrors of what a supposedly Christian country did to Jews in mid-20th century (while all too many Christians elsewhere looked on silently), by the renaissance of many of the world's religions, and by the movements of Buddhist, Hindu, Muslim and Sikh immigrants into Europe and North America.

The WCC's second assembly in 1954 recognized the link between renascent religions and nationalism in many areas, as it commissioned a study on "The Word of God and the Living Faiths of Men". Convinced that Christians share a common humanity and an equal place in the love of God with persons of other faiths, and that respectful encounter may help all believers understand their own traditions better, the WCC called its first consultation on interfaith dialogue in 1967. Four years later its subunit on Dialogue was created, placing the accent on actual meeting and conversation with persons of each faith. *Guidelines on Dialogue* approved by the central committee in 1979 stressed the need to set such dialogue in an experience of community.

Inevitably this practice of dialogue has raised with greater intensity the question of how Christians should best view the place of people of other faiths within the activity of God in history. This is no abstract, theoretical question. The *Guidelines* note that it must be asked "in terms of what God may be doing in the lives of hundreds of millions of men and women who live in and seek community together with Christians, but along different ways". Despite the elusiveness of ecumenical consensus the WCC has helped to keep this question on the churches' agenda.

Meanwhile, the WCC has pursued three other interlocking tasks within its interfaith relationships:

• *Organizing formal encounters between Christians and people of other religious traditions.* Many of these have been jointly planned between the WCC and representative leaders and partners of a particular faith community, less often involving several faith communities at the same time. Such encounters usually focus on a specific topic of common concern. Dialogues of this sort have been held jointly with Buddhists, Hindus, Muslims and Jews; less often there have also been contacts with Sikhs, Jains, Confucians and adherents of traditional religion in Africa, North America and the Pacific.

Again and again those who participate in interfaith encounters – Christians and their partners alike – testify that dialogue enriches those who take part in it. This may be a matter of new intellectual insights, or of deepened theological understanding, although all stress that dialogue is not intended to be an exercise in comparative religion. Yet more important is the enrichment of spirituality that often takes place in such encounters.

There are also obstacles to dialogue. Christians who come from places where religious pluralism is not an everyday reality may rank dialogue low among their priorities. Others remain sceptical about the entire enterprise: explicitly or implicitly they ask what they have to gain from dialogue, especially if they have been brought up to suppose that other religions are "primitive" or "pagan". On the other hand, the partners of the other faiths may suspect that dialogue is a stalking horse for Christian evangelism.

In some cases, the effectiveness of dialogue is diminished by a reluctance to raise hard questions of the partner, to search for common ground while carefully avoiding any confrontation over possibly controversial issues.

Each dialogue has its own context, objectives and ongoing issues. At the international level, Christian-Jewish dialogue is the most organized, with the WCC working in collaboration with the International Jewish Committee for Interreligious Consultations. More recent are the relationships developed with international Islamic organizations.

• *Encouraging and enabling churches to be in dialogue in their own contexts*. The test of the validity of such models of interfaith relationships-in-community at the international level is the extent to which they are picked up, reflected and made productive in local situations.

In some places people of different faiths share a common struggle against suffering and oppression: Muslim and Christian Palestinians, for example; or Buddhists, Confucianists and Christians in Korea during the Japanese occupation. This can provide a more profound experience of interfaith solidarity than formal dialogue. Yet all too often, once the crisis has passed, faith communities go their separate ways.

In countries that were colonies until a generation ago, cooperation across religious lines may have proved a resource for nation-building. Just how this happens has differed according to the way the new state understands itself – as a secular state, for instance, or as incorporating a national religion. Even in officially secular countries many people – Hindus in India, or Christians in the USA, for example – believe their own religion should be considered *the* religion of the nation as a whole.

In areas where churches founded by foreign missionaries have been slow to indigenize, they may continue to be identified with the colonialism of the past and the Western economic dominance of the present. Even aid distributed by Christian agencies to all sections of the population can have an ambiguous effect on interfaith relations, especially if it is felt to be supporting resistance to social change.

In many situations a good deal of mistrust must be overcome before dialogue can begin. Religious differences are often linked to the quest for political power. Theological conservatism and fears about preserving the identity of a minority community may also lead Christians or members of other faiths to oppose dialogue.

Questions of religious freedom and of majority-minority relations often arise. This is especially true in Muslim-Christian relationships: in West Africa, for instance, where some areas have Muslim majorities, others Christian; in the Middle East, where historic but long-since-minority Christian communities live in a largely Muslim environment; or in Western Europe, with its recently arrived communities of migrant workers from Turkey, Pakistan, Bangladesh or North Africa.

• *Ensuring that the perspectives of other faiths are taken into account in WCC activities.* It was at the WCC's fifth assembly in Nairobi in 1975 that persons of other faiths were for the first time invited to attend an assembly as guests, and one of them addressed the Assembly. In the later assemblies the number and participation of such guests has increased. Their presence reminds delegates of the reality of pluralism, encourages a commitment to listening, and reveals that people of other faiths often share many of the concerns of WCC churches.

Attempts have been made to extend this symbolic presence of people of other faiths to the WCC's ongoing programme work. One area has been the growing emphasis on preservation of the environment. Both in terms of understanding creation, nature and humanity and in terms of practical commitments to reverse the ravages of ecological degradation, interfaith encounter and cooperation is not only valuable but necessary. Another example is the situation of women and the ways male-dominated interpretations of religious traditions reinforce the oppression of women.

The title of the WCC dialogue programme originally spoke of "people of living faiths *and ideologies*". An ideology was understood, in the words of an early consultation on the subject, as "a system of thought or blueprint used to interpret society and to legitimate existing structures or to change them".

The ideology with the highest profile in the 20th century was Marxism. Both the power which Marxist political parties exercised over much of the world's population and the suspicion of some in the West that the WCC was too much influenced by Marxism lent urgency to Christian-Marxist dialogue in the first forty years of the WCC's life.

Yet any such dialogue was complicated by the attitude of those Marxist parties to religion and by the resulting – and diverse – positions of WCC member churches in Marxist countries. These difficulties were heightened by the Soviet invasion of Czechoslovakia in 1968. Between these directly political difficulties, the sensitivity of looking for ways of dialogue with Marxists in a situation where few intellectual leaders wanted to accept that identity, and indeed the amount of work which the small WCC staff teams were finding so eagerly welcomed among their partners of other religions, Christian-Marxist dialogue in an internationally organized sense could never achieve prominence with the WCC. Member churches in Cuba and China continued to work for mutual understanding with their governments, and to live out their Christian commitment in their evolving societies, but seldom made Christian-Marxist dialogue a priority.

The changes that swept over Central and Eastern Europe towards the end of the 1980s have altered the situation and the atmosphere for the churches in those lands. The loss of political power and credibility by Marxist parties in one country after another meant that dialogue with Marxism – which had hardly existed anyway – moved more or less totally off the priority list of the churches there. They have many more urgent challenges and opportunities to occupy them. Some church leaders there have spoken of the impor-

WCC general secretary Konrad Raiser during a visit to the Democratic People's Republic of Korea in April 1999. With him are Park Kyung Seo, WCC secretary for Asia, and Kang Yong-Sop and Hwang Min-Woo, respectively president and director of international affairs of the Korean Christian Federation

tance of reflection on their experiences under Marxism; some have also stressed that neither the human values which Marxists claimed to be promoting nor the lessons learned by the churches in those circumstances should be lost, whatever the enthusiasm to embrace the market economy.

Secular groups and organizations

Finally, we need to look at relationships the Council pursues with other organizations and groups.

Governments

With member churches in over one hundred countries, the WCC finds it difficult to generalize about church-state relationships. Relationships vary enormously, and are always changing.

Some WCC member churches are officially recognized as *the* church of their country, often receiving money from or through the government and performing a variety of civil service functions. Less officially, other churches know themselves as folk churches which, by their size and tradition, consider themselves to be the church of their nation, whether or not the state has any part in their governance. In countries where church and state are constitutionally separate, some churches may consider themselves "mainline", custodians of national symbols to which political authorities need to listen. In yet other areas churches are tolerated, perhaps because they are too small to cause problems and intolerance would be too high a price for an image-conscious government to pay. Elsewhere churches may be prevented from doing any evangelism in public, educating children and young people, or engaging in any activity that calls the status quo into question. In a few places, despite constitutional guarantees of religious freedom, churches have to live under persecution.

This range of church-state relationships creates a diversity in the WCC's relationships with governments. A government's relationship with its own churches must always be taken into consideration by the WCC, for example when considering how best to deal with reports of human-rights violations.

Normally the WCC does not mediate directly in international conflicts. Yet its experience, worldwide contacts and past record of service in a given situation can enable it to open lines of communication between warring parties, or to influence world opinion by helping create a climate of confidence for negotiations.

Some WCC programmes for development, education and refugees have been supported by government funds. This raises delicate issues, for the Council and for the governments alike. Yet ecumenical structures can offer an effective means of channelling aid that would be difficult for governments to send any other way. At the same time the WCC must acknowledge that many of its larger projects would have been impossible to fund without the help of governments.

Intergovernmental organizations

Through its Commission of the Churches on International Affairs (CCIA) the WCC has official status with the United Nations. At the annual sessions of the UN Commission on

Human Rights the WCC usually presents testimony on behalf of certain member churches.

Several other WCC units have had their own relationships with UN agencies. The Christian Medical Commission, for example, worked closely with the World Health Organization, the WCC Refugee Service with the UN High Commissioner for Refugees. The WCC has played a signifcant role in drawing the attention of its member churches to particular emphases within the UN system, such as the proclamation of special "Years" for children, disabled persons, uprooted people and others.

Non-governmental organizations

Many other NGOs affiliated with the UN have interests which overlap with those of the WCC. So the Council will often exchange information and share in some endeavour with them, both at the international level and within a particular area of the world.

The media

Contacts between the WCC and the media have often been the source of misunderstanding over the years, even if at one level many of the interests of the ecumenical movement would seem to coincide, or at least be compatible, with the ideals of the media.

As modern media and their technologies have evolved, most of the images and information that enlarge people's perception of world realities are transmitted chiefly through the media. Newspaper reporters and combat photographers, bringing home the horrors of battle to people far from the front, have done a great deal to erase the glories of war. Television especially was able to mobilize worldwide response to the suffering caused by drought and famine in Africa in the mid-1980s. Photographs of the earth taken from the moon and broadcast around the globe are among the most eloquent symbols of humanity's common destiny on a precious but fragile planet. Moreover the link between the media and the possibilities of human freedom and dignity is evident in the

A team of experts discussing the plan for a new hospital in Pucarani, on the Altiplano in Bolivia

tight control of the media that oppressive regimes invariably impose.

Despite this common concern, the WCC often finds itself the object of media criticism and suspicion. Journalists may misunderstand, or find uninteresting, the spiritual and theological dimensions of the church and the ecumenical movement, and may disregard any talk of the transcendent as outside the scope of their coverage. They may consider the pronouncements of the churches as merely romantic idealism which has little to do with the real world. They may insist that the WCC and its member churches should not be exempt from the close scrutiny it is their business to apply to governments and businesses, schools and trade unions. They may resent criticism by church people of the media or of the systems that give them power and privilege. They may simply be serving masters who look with disfavour on people who try to tell the truth about the dominant powers in today's world.

Nevertheless, the WCC remains committed to partnership with the public media, and puts much effort into helping them report accurately what it is doing. Its own resources for communicating the story of the ecumenical community in the many countries, languages and cultures of today are limited. Since the voice of most of its member churches is small and weak too, the WCC must do its best to see that the secular media pick up on its activities and spread the news of at least some of what it is doing. Because of their various presuppositions and priorities, the media will seldom tell the story in exactly the way the WCC would wish; yet when they are unfairly critical of the WCC their independence will persuade many people, including church members, that their account is the correct one.

Since its beginnings, the WCC has tried to be transparent about its activities, programmes and decision-making processes. With few exceptions – when particular persons are being discussed, or when disclosure could put people's lives or safety at risk – plenary sessions of the assembly and the central committee are open to accredited media representatives. Press operations, with news conferences and interview opportunities, are organized at all major meetings.

The WCC has also spoken up about communication as an essential component of the struggle for freedom, justice and peace. With others in the ecumenical movement, the WCC has encouraged churches and their members, including those who are media professionals, to give attention to how their work can be used to build or to break down human community.

* * *

These various sides of the question about the WCC's relationships all show how in one way or another the Council's relationships can help to extend the influence of the ecumenical movement and the causes to which the churches together have committed themselves. The matter of relationships, in other words, is inevitably bound up with issues of power.

The danger in highlighting this is that it might lead us to miss the key ecumenical vocation of empowering the powerless, the victims of the "powers of this age", those whose lives are shaped and determined not by God's gifts to them but by the decisions of other people – including some powers with which the WCC entertains relationships. It is this calling which compels the churches, today as in every earlier

time, to open themselves to those God gives them as neighbours, however different or demanding, in order to create a
foretaste of the universally inclusive community which Jesus
promised, when "people will come from East and West, from
South and North, to sit at table in the Kingdom of God"
(Luke 13:29).

5. Thinking Together in Faith

To ensure thorough preparation for one of the eight sections of the 1910 world missionary conference in Edinburgh, John R. Mott, its chairman, wrote letters to some six hundred missionaries, asking them questions about the appropriate attitudes for Christians entering into contact with people of other world faiths. Advance materials for the Life and Work movement's Oxford conference of 1937 filled seven published volumes. For a draft towards the main theme of the WCC's second assembly of 1954, "Christ, the Hope of the World", the Council brought together twenty-five of "the most creative thinkers of the churches" for three stormy sessions.

Many other examples of deliberate "study processes" within the WCC could be mentioned. For the ecumenical movement has always known that rigorous and imaginative thinking is indispensable. Time was, observes Swedish theologian Krister Stendhal, when "the list of participants in conferences read like a 'Who's Who' of influential bishops and theologians" – and many of the bishops themselves were theologians of note.

By no means were clergy the only thinkers enlisted in the cause. An outspoken advocate of leadership from among lay Christians was Joseph H. Oldham, first general secretary of the International Missionary Council. Known for his instinct for what he called "first-class minds", Oldham often convened informal groups of philosophers, scientists, sociologists – and also poets – for intensive discussion. This was no mere brainstorming; it was a strategy for addressing what Oldham saw as the life-and-death question for the church: how to enable Christians to respond to a secular civilization.

Oldham's vision of the future World Council of Churches, says Visser 't Hooft, emphasized "the importance of study and research... sometimes even calling this its main function. The churches needed the help of the "ablest minds", and the process of common thinking had to be so organized that these could be used to best advantage."

The importance the ecumenical movement has given to building up and building upon an intellectual tradition makes eminent sense, given that churches have often been divided over theological ideas and depended on the intellectual contribution of their theologians. As we have seen, the WCC has no constitutional authority over its members. The intrinsic "truth and wisdom" of ecumenical declarations is their only source of influence, so the best possible intellectual work is needed to give weight to what is said.

The WCC's audience is not only churches, its subject matter is not only theology. As a 1937 statement of what a future WCC should be like put it: "The witness which the church in the modern world is called to give is such that in certain spheres the predominant voice in the utterance of it must be that of lay people holding posts of responsibility and influence in the secular world... A first-class intelligence staff is indispensable."

Now of course the WCC is not the only place where ecumenical thinking is pursued. Bilateral theological dialogues between worldwide Christian communions are playing a key role in the thinking of the ecumenical movement, complementing the multilateral discussions in the WCC.

In some places, ecumenical study centres or institutes have been founded. A contribution to relations between Christians and people of other faiths came from Christian study centres promoted by the International Missionary Council. "Lay academies" in Germany and elsewhere have provided places for ecumenical thinking on many contemporary issues. Specialized societies often focus on specific topics, such as the questions facing couples in the Association of Inter-Church Families. As theological faculties increasingly involve people of different churches, theological and biblical scholarship is often ecumenically in the vanguard.

Yet this emphasis on the need for solid ecumenical thinking is not without its risks. Four temptations call for vigilance.

• *Elitism:* Intellectuals generally enjoy a certain prestige in society, and despite the churches' commitment to equality, it is not immune from temptation in this area. In recognizing the value of drawing on "first-class minds", the ecumenical movement no less needs to value the thought and convictions of others.

• *Provincialism:* The determination of what makes for a "first-class mind" rests, of course, on certain criteria, almost always drawn from the Western intellectual tradition. This is why the WCC is constantly drawing in people from other areas of human civilization.

• *Selectivity:* Stendhal points out that when drawing on intellectual contributions in fields other than those of theology, there is a temptation "to choose those voices which seem to fit best into one's theological scheme of things", i.e. to enlist only those "who can supply arguments in support of pre-conceived positions".

• *Immobility:* Yet there is the opposite pitfall. Christians may conclude from thorough intellectual investigation of some situation or issue that there are so many ambiguities and uncertainties that any action in response will be tainted, and so best avoided. This is the dilemma pointed to in Marx's famous remark that while philosophers try to interpret the world, the real point is to *change* it.

A lastingly influential model

In the 1970s there was much talk in the WCC about the "action/reflection" model emerging from Latin America, by which shared *thinking* is devoted to discerning the most appropriate *action*, whose results in turn prompt yet more careful *thinking*. José Míguez Bonino, a leading Argentinian theologian, points out that the churches often decide that "something must be done" about some problem in society, not because of their theology or social analysis but rather from "a sort of intuitive awareness" or "prophetic discernment". Such action, in turn, will often become a fruitful subject for subsequent theological reflection.

Míguez points out that this action/reflection process has often led the WCC to fresh theological convictions. Rejection of racism and sexism, and the call for the church to stand in solidarity with the poor, he says, are three examples of what may genuinely be described as an "ecumenical consensus". To be sure, there is no universal agreement about the precise theological status of these convictions or about their specific ethical implications. Yet "whatever the nuances and differences, no church today can ignore these issues; all churches involved in the ecumenical movement recognize themselves as theologically and ethically accountable in this respect".

This action/reflection model can thus help to overcome "the paralysis of analysis". Yet it may also lead to what Míguez calls "functional theologies", in which people use terms like "incarnation" or "kingdom of God" to legitimate some social action but make no corresponding effort to "enrich, purify and correct" their action by theological reflection on these concepts.

A wide range of studies

A list drawn up in 1981 suggested that in its first 35 years the WCC had made some sixty "major" studies, though this does not include many significant studies of less scope. Any brief attempt to survey the literally hundreds of studies undertaken by the WCC since 1948 can do little more than hint at the range of issues to which this ecumenical agency has devoted sustained intellectual attention.

Most early studies built on the intellectual heritage of Faith and Order, Life and Work (now known as Church and Society) and – after 1961 – World Mission and Evangelism. Until 1971 there was a separate Division of Studies within the WCC. Robert Bilheimer, its director in the 1960s, says a separate division was established because Visser 't Hooft feared that otherwise the pressures of increased activity would lead to neglect of this historic function, and the dissipation of the intellectual thrust of the ecumenical tradition.

Among studies that have made a lasting impact on the ecumenical tradition and the WCC were three ventures in articulating a social vision for the church. Their successive themes – "The Responsible Society", "Rapid Social Change" and "Faith and Science in an Unjust World" – echoed down the first thirty years of the WCC as the ecumenical movement sought to discern the churches' appropriate response to the capitalist and socialist economies, while also helping its member churches in the post-colonialist tasks of nation-building, and dealing with the new challenges arising from scientific and technological progress.

Ground-breaking studies of more classically theological questions included Faith and Order's investigations of "Scripture, Tradition and Traditions", "Worship in Secular Age", and the twin studies "God in Nature and History" and "Man in Nature and History". An influential reflection on the mission of the church in an age when "the mission field" came to mean all six continents was "The Missionary Structure of the Congregation".

From more recent years, let us take a quick look at four different, yet usefully inter-related study processes.

• The study on "The Community of Women and Men in the Church" of the late 1970s and early 1980s was notable for its pioneering method of inviting local groups to provide raw material for theological and policy reflection by working

Young women operate a word processor with 3000 characters at the Amity Foundation printing press, near Nanjing, China

through a study guide published in Geneva. Following regional meetings and two consultations on specific issues raised in these local responses, an international consultation in Sheffield, UK, in 1981 produced a number of recommendations for the WCC. The effects of this study in challenging male domination and encouraging fuller partnerships of men and women are still ringing with good news in many places.

Historically, this study stands in a line that reaches back to the beginnings of the WCC with the research and 1952 report on "the service and status of women in the church". Another key moment was the 1974 consultation in Berlin on "Sexism in the 1970s". The Community study was located, for administrative purposes, in Faith and Order; many of the issues it raised have been taken further in Faith and Order's study process on "The Unity of the Church and the Renewal of Human Community".

• During the 1980s the WCC's Christian Medical Commission carried out an extensive study on how Christians can best understand *health, healing and wholeness*. Here too an effort was made to secure contributions from all over the world. This was done through ten regional consultations, involving health and social workers, pastors and chaplains to share ideas, experiences and insights. Beside contributing to ecumenical rethinking of the church's healing ministry – arising from "medical missions" – and bringing a new emphasis on preventive health care, these meetings built networks among people facing new challenges in their regions.

• Following the sixth assembly (Vancouver 1983), the WCC made encouraging the churches to covenant together in mutual commitment to "justice, peace and the integrity of creation" a priority. "Integrity of creation" was a new phrase in the WCC lexicon, for the issues it raised – the implications of Christian faith for the environmental crisis – had received little attention in the ecumenical movement. In the late 1980s consultations brought Christian theologians together with scientists, representatives of indigenous peoples, and thinkers from other world faiths.

The early stages of this study, as often happens, served largely to make Christians aware of the complexity and breadth of the issues. Clearly, there could be no easy arrival at an ecumenical consensus. Yet it soon became clear that a common charge – that Christian readings of the Genesis mandate to "subdue the earth" have been a major factor in environmental destruction – should be met with further reflection on the Christian doctrine of creation. Signs of a reorientation have included church efforts to get the threat of climate change taken seriously, and a movement of "eco-congregations", which build environmental concern into their activities.

• Starting from a first conference with scientists in 1970, whose thinking led to the 1979 world conference on "Faith, Science and the Future", held at the Massachussetts Institute of Technology, the WCC's Church and Society sub-unit pin-pointed genetics as one of the crucial fields deserving careful

As the trend to patent high-yielding, disease-resistant seeds cloned in first-world laboratories grows, small farmers in third-world countries may be forced to pay a fee instead of simply saving some of this year's harvest for next year's planting

ethical reflection. In 1989 the central committee sent to all member churches the report *Bio-technology: Its Challenges to the Churches and the World* which discusses ethical dilemmas that few Christians could have imagined twenty years earlier.

Six major areas are highlighted: human genetic engineering, reproductive technology, intellectual property rights, environmental effects, military applications, and the impact of bio-technology on the third world. The report recognizes what agonising choices can confront individuals and corporate bodies in these fields, thus adding complex new dimensions to the pastoral role of church leaders and individual Christians. For in all these areas, let alone others which will be opened up in the future, technology is by no means an unalloyed benefit to humanity. For example, the bio-technological development in laboratories of the flavour of "natural" vanilla could eliminate any need to grow the actual vanilla bean – and thus deprive Madagascar, which grows three-quarters of the world's supply, of tens of millions of dollars a year. Still more, "the whole future of seeds is at stake", as subsequent events involving the powerful US multinational firm Monsanto have vividly shown.

Time alone will tell whether the WCC's alerting of the churches will have made a significant contribution to the necessary and unprecedented regulation of bio-technological "advance". But the report was surely an important warning; indeed one of its strongest recommendations was that churches, scientists and international and non-governmental organizations should hold regular consultations on the "political evolution of bio-technology and its impact on global justice".

Two long-lasting concerns

Two other studies have special importance.

1. Baptism, Eucharist and Ministry: a classical theological study

With half a million copies distributed in thirty languages, this is probably the best-known of all WCC studies. Few of the meetings organized by Faith and Order since its first world gathering in 1927 have not had one or another of these classic church-dividing issues on their agenda. Unwillingness to recognize the validity of each other's baptism, celebration of the Lord's supper, or ordained ministry is one of the most obvious indications of church division. No visible unity can be achieved without agreement on these three areas.

It was in 1971 that a first attempt was made to summarize the results of the many discussions and reports on different facets of the church dividing issues connected with baptism and with the Lord's Supper, now commonly called the "eucharist" (the Greek word for "thanksgiving"). These seemed so promising that the Faith and Order commission, at its meeting in 1974 in Accra, Ghana, prepared a draft text on baptism, eucharist and ministry. The 1975 fifth assembly in Nairobi found this so promising that it sent the document to all member churches and partner bodies for comment. More than a hundred churches sent in detailed suggestions. Analysis of these and a series of consultations on the more difficult areas led to submission of a revised text to the commission at its 1982 meeting in Lima. After some final revisions there, the Vancouver assembly of 1983 submitted it to the churches for "an official response to this text at the highest appropriate level of authority". The assembly asked for statements on: the extent to which your church can recognize in this text the faith of the church through the ages; the consequences your church can draw from this text for its relations and dialogues with other churches...; the guidance your church can take from this text for its worship, educational, ethical and spiritual life and witness; the suggestions your church can make for the ongoing work of Faith and Order.

Both the wide distribution of the Lima text and the reactions to it (almost 200 official church responses, with perhaps five times as many evaluations and commentaries from groups and individuals) came as a surprise to those who thought that doctrinal issues could arouse little interest in the churches or that the WCC had lost interest in theology.

The Lima text is all the more significant because the Faith and Order commission includes representatives from churches not in membership of the Council, among them officially appointed Roman Catholic members. Yet there are three common misconceptions to clear up:

• The Lima text is not a complete ecumenical theology of baptism, eucharist and ministry; it is rather a text concentrating on the aspects of those issues which have caused church division.

• While expressing what its preface calls "a remarkable degree of agreement", the Lima text (often referred to as BEM) is not a "consensus statement". The agreements to which it points are clearly not enough "to realize and maintain the church's visible unity". Rather than "consensus" the text speaks of "convergences" which appear as churches "leave behind the hostilities of the past" and recognize how much they have in common in their understanding of the faith. The Lima text is an attempt to reflect this doctrinal convergence.

• Valuable as it is, doctrinal agreement on baptism, eucharist and ministry is only one part of the long road towards unity. Within Faith and Order, BEM takes its place alongside two other major studies – one on the common understanding and confession of the apostolic faith, the other on the inseparability of the search for church unity from the quest for renewed human community. The formulation of doctrinal agreements "cannot be divorced from the redemptive and liberating mission of Christ through the churches in the modern world".

With these considerations in mind, the churches were asked to respond to the Lima text, not with the expectation that it be revised yet again, but to suggest ways BEM might "lead to acts of unity, deepening of relationships and community of witness", as the Faith and Order commission said in 1989.

BEM has grown out of, and itself opened up a further worldwide process. Yet the language of the text is largely that of classical theology, since most of the divisions over these three topics are rooted in old controversies in Europe. Although the majority of the responses sent in have been positive, they also show that these old controversies remain alive. This is hardly surprising, since the exposure to other Christian traditions that is at the heart of the ecumenical movement often leads to a deeper understanding and appreciation of one's own tradition. Yet the hope remains that the new context in which the BEM process sets this discussion will help to break down the church-dividing character of these differences.

So let us look more closely at some of the key points on each of the three issues:

Baptism "unites us to Christ in faith", says the BEM text, yet it has led to disunity among Christ's followers when churches have refused to recognize each other's baptismal practices, or allowed "differences of sex, race or social status to divide the body of Christ".

Is the well-known argument over "infant" or "believer's" baptism irreconcilable? The Lima text points to a fundamental agreement underlying both forms of baptism: they "embody God's own initiative in Christ and express a response of faith made within the believing community".

Within this common understanding, the accents fall differently. Infant baptism emphasizes "the corporate faith and the faith which the child shares with its parents... Through baptism the promise and claim of the gospel are laid upon the child." Believer's baptism stresses "the explicit confession of the person who responds to the grace of God in and through the community of faith and who seeks baptism".

Whatever the form, "the personal faith of the recipient of baptism and faithful participation in the life of the church are essential for the full fruit of baptism". That is why baptism should be celebrated within the setting of the Christian community and linked to a commitment to continuing Christian nurture for the person baptized.

On another divisive issue, "re-baptism", the Lima text is unequivocal. "Baptism is an unrepeatable act" and "any practice which might be interpreted as 're-baptism' must be

A baptism in a Russian Orthodox church in Novosibirsk

avoided". But baptism does need to be "constantly re-affirmed".

The document calls for further study of three social and cultural issues connected with baptism: its connection with giving people "Christian" names which are not rooted in their own cultural tradition; apparently "indiscriminate" baptism by large "majority" churches in the West; and the practice of baptism of the Holy Spirit without water, through the laying-on of hands.

The *eucharist* is one complete act which includes "thanksgiving to the Father, memorial of Christ, invocation of the Spirit, communion of the faithful, meal of the kingdom". On one historically divisive issue, the Lima text encourages churches "to review the old controversies about 'sacrifice' in the light of the biblical conception of memorial".

Another area of theological dispute has been over the connection between bread and wine and the presence of Christ in the eucharist. There have been "various attempts to understand the mystery" of this presence. Noting that "Christ fulfills in a variety of ways his promise to be always with his own even to the end of the world", the text describes his mode of presence in the eucharist as unique, real, living and active.

One paragraph in the Lima document links the eucharist with social, economic and political life. "All kinds of injustice, racism, separation and lack of freedom are radically

challenged when we share in the body and blood of Christ...
As participants in the eucharist, we prove inconsistent if we
are not actively participating in the ongoing restoration of the
world's situation and the human condition."

Ministry: Remarkable as the doctrinal convergences on
the eucharist expressed in the Lima text undoubtedly are,
they cannot yet come to full ecumenical expression in the life
of the church largely because of longstanding and persistent
differences about the ordained ministry. In short, agreement
on who may preside at the celebration of the eucharist seems
still to be far off. There are thus grounds for affirming that
the most serious divergences between the Christian confessions occur at the point of the commissioning – through calling on the Holy Spirit and the laying-on of hands – their
ordained ministers.

The Lima text pleads with the churches, first to give full
weight to the fact that they are united in their affirmation of
God's calling to his church *as a whole*: "The Holy Spirit
unites in a single body those who follow Jesus Christ and
sends them as witnesses into the world."

Second, BEM asks the churches to remember that the
point of church order is that "the gospel be spread and the
community built up in love", and that they "avoid attributing
their particular forms of the ordained ministry directly to the
will and institution of Jesus Christ".

The text says "there is no single New Testament pattern"
(of the ordained ministry), the Spirit has often led the church
to adapt its ministries to particular needs and "the threefold
ministry of bishop, presbyter and deacon may today serve as
an expression of the unity we seek and also as a means of
achieving it". Yet, it says that this threefold pattern is "in
need of reform", especially where collegiality among the
bishops has been obscured.

The Lima text does not seek to resolve another ecumenically controversial issue – the ordination of women. It notes
that churches which ordain women do so on the basis of the
conviction "that the ordained ministry of the church lacks
fullness when it is limited to one sex". And it says this con-

viction "has been reinforced by their experience during the years in which they have included women in their ordained ministries".

On the other hand, "those churches which do not practise the ordination of women consider that the force of nineteen centuries of tradition against the ordination of women must not be set aside. They believe that such a tradition cannot be dismissed as a lack of respect for the participation of women in the church. They believe that there are theological issues concerning the nature of humanity and concerning Christology which lie at the heart of their convictions and understanding of the role of women in the church."

While such differences hinder the mutual recognition of ministries, says the text, they do not prevent further efforts towards such recognition. "Openness to each other holds the possibility that the Spirit may well speak to one church through the insights of another. Ecumenical consideration, therefore, should encourage, not restrain, the facing of this question."

All churches confess that the church is to be "apostolic". Yet there is disagreement on how this relates to the particular task of the ordained ministry "of preserving and actualizing the apostolic faith". One of the ways this was expressed in the early church was through the succession of bishops. Churches which retain this practice are increasingly acknowledging that "continuity in apostolic faith, worship and mission has been preserved in churches which have not retained the form of historic episcopate". At the same time, many of those churches "are expressing willingness to accept episcopal succession as a sign of the apostolicity of the life of the whole church", although they cannot agree that their own ministry is invalid until it enters this line of "episcopal succession".

Responses. The responses to the Lima text have made it clear that considerable theological study of baptism, eucharist and especially ministry remains to be done – and done together in ecumenical fellowship. As a "convergence text" – the Faith and Order commission noted in its 1989 meeting – "BEM calls neither for surrender, nor compromise, nor total acceptance, and certainly not for ambiguity or confusion. It calls rather for common affirmations by divided churches struggling towards universal communion." Among the continuing areas of difficulty in that struggle are the relationships between word and sacrament, and between scripture and Tradition, understanding of sacraments and sacramentality, the ministry of women and of men, succession in ordained ministry, and the nature and purpose of the church.

2. Economic justice

This area of debate and research has also been a constant and vitally important element in the ecumenical movement for many generations. Already in the 1920s, the British Conference on Christian Politics, Economics and Citizenship, called by a committee chaired by the future Archbishop William Temple to prepare for the Stockholm Life and Work conference, insisted that for Christians the concept of service should come before that of profit, industry should serve the needs of the community, and unemployment and extremes of poverty and wealth were morally unacceptable. In 1928 the Jerusalem conference of the International Missionary Council asked for a department of social and industrial research as "a necessary and highly important arm of the missionary enterprise".

By the time of the Oxford conference (1937), attention was focused particularly on the competing totalitarianisms of communism and fascism. Both offered specific recipes for economic "salvation", yet both were sharply criticized by the Oxford meeting. At the founding assembly of the WCC (1948) it was the competing "concentrations of power" in laissez-faire capitalism and communism which were the focus of attention:

> The Christian churches should reject the ideologies of both... and should seek to draw men away from the false assumption that these extremes are the only alternatives.... It is the responsibility of Christians to seek new, creative solutions which never allow either justice or freedom to destroy the other.

A key chapter opened in the 1960s with the arrival in ecumenical debates of strong voices from the churches in the so-called under-developed countries of the South. Church and Society's project on "rapid social change" could not avoid the hard questions to do with economic power in the formerly colonial areas, and at its world conference in Geneva (1966) many sharp questions were raised about the difficulties of achieving any justice between the different "worlds" on the one planet. The Uppsala assembly (1968) took two major steps, by establishing the Commission on the Churches' Participation in Development (CCPD) (whose first meeting laid down three interacting goals: justice, self-reliance and economic growth), and by launching the Programme to Combat Racism with a Special Fund to be constituted by a proportion of the WCC's financial reserves: member churches were invited to offer significant comparable monies of their own, so that the Fund could make gifts without strings to those struggling for justice against racism. Both of these triggered heated debates on economic ethics in several churches.

Preparation for the struggles of the 21st century may perhaps have begun in the later 1970s with a study by the CCPD, drawing on the liberation theology from Latin America, "Towards a Church in Solidarity with the Poor". This led to three successive volumes, which all opened up perspectives "through the eyes of the poor", a phrase corresponding to the Roman Catholic emphasis on "God's preferential option for the poor". This phrase has significantly transformed the mind-set of many within the churches, particularly those of the "rich, white West" who have heard in it an evangelical call to solidarity with their partners in the South.

Thus, during the 1980s the WCC's Advisory Group on Economic Matters addressed itself to the challenges of a New International Economic Order, the nature and effects of transnational corporations, world hunger and the international financial system – all illustrating the apparently unbreakable grip held by the rich on and over the many unalterably poor countries. In 1992 the central committee circulated to all member churches the study document *Christian Faith and the World Economy Today*, which sought to provide an overview for Christians and churches of the key questions of the day, using as the essential criteria four "signposts" from the biblical tradition:

1) the essential goodness of the created order, and humanity's responsibility for it;

2) the innate value and freedom of each human being and of all humanity;

3) God's concern, and the covenant in Christ, with all humankind, breaking through whatever barriers we build between us;

4) God's justice as the over-arching standard for interhuman relationships and behaviour – to be discovered through a "preferential option for the poor".

This approach flowered in the 1990s in the Jubilee 2000 movement for the cancellation of the unpayable debts of the 52 most indebted countries. This was eagerly taken up, both

During the "Geneva 2000" social summit, an ecumenical team was part of a non-governmental organization demonstration to "drop the debt"　　　　　　　　　　　　　　　　　　WCC/Catherine Alt

in richer and in poorer countries, by churches and other NGOs, and was warmly endorsed by the Harare assembly (1998), but failed to find significant response in the circles of the International Monetary Fund and World Bank, so that the new millennium dawned with at best 21 countries having received relief on a small proportion of their debts.

Harare put that campaign – along with much else – within the context of a call to face up to the vast challenge of what the secular world calls "globalization":

> The emergence... of transnational and increasingly world-wide structures of communication, finance and economy [which have] created a particular kind of global unity, whose cost is growing fragmentation for societies and exclusion for more and more of the human family.... Economic globalization is guided by the neo-liberal ideology... that through competing economic forces and purposes an "invisible hand" will assure the optimum good as every individual person pursues his or her economic gain.... This globalized oikoumene of domination is in contrast with the oikoumene of faith and solidarity that motivates and energizes the ecumenical movement. The logic of globalization needs to be challenged by an alternative way of life of community in diversity....

That call was given flesh in several recommendations, including far-reaching reform of the current economic structures and practices, and renewed emphasis on

> local alternatives through new forms of organizing production, fair trade, alternative banking systems and – particularly in highly industrialized countries – changes in life-style and consumption patterns.

The Harare paper on globalization suggested "four essentials for a life-centred vision to be nurtured":

> participation as the optimal inclusion of all involved at all levels; equity as basic fairness that also extends to other life-forms; accountability as the structuring of responsibility towards one another and earth itself; and sufficiency as the commitment to meet basic needs of all life possible and develop a quality of life that includes bread for all but is more than bread alone.

The basic meaning of "economics" is "the management of the resources of the household". It is not purely to do with money, even if the more "developed" our societies become the more we become dominated by, obsessed with and dependent on the monetary system we have ourselves created. Yet the "household of humanity" consists essentially of one another, the full community of humankind, together with the planet on which we live and on whose health and life-supporting potentialities we depend.

Towards a vital and coherent theology

This chapter has been trying to illustrate and to some extent summarize the wide range of concerns that come onto the agenda of the World Council of Churches. Taking up any of these issues will involve listening to a surprisingly wide and never predictable range of voices, and then trying to synthesize them to develop an ecumenical approach to church action.

The Council's critics often deplore the millions of words that are exchanged, written down and – sometimes – published, in the course of its work. Of course a good deal in the exchanges turns out to be inappropriate, just as not a few of the resulting documents prove unmemorable and soon go out of date. No single publication can ever be the last word; each generation of church leaders, important as it no doubt is for them to study the findings of their predecessors, must come to their own judgments. Since, as the Vancouver assembly of 1983 put it, "there never will be a time when the world, with all its political, social and economic issues, ceases to be the agenda of the church", it is inevitable that the WCC will continue to study a considerable range of subjects.

Those who observe the Council's work from outside often ask what, if anything, holds it all together. Does not the fact that quite separate groups and committees handle different topics in very different ways mean that there can be inconsistencies and even disagreements between separate studies? By the same token, since no such study group can in practice be adequately representative of all the member churches, in what sense can the WCC claim to speak for all?

What guarantee is there that any particular text has not been hi-jacked by one part of the Council membership?

The constitutional answer to this latter question points to the central committee and the assembly as the bodies which are to be as representative as possible. As this chapter has mentioned, the more important study reports are brought to a meeting of the central committee to test if there is sufficient agreement for them to be officially sent round to all member churches and partner bodies. Many less crucial texts are published in one of the Council's journals or books, or circulated as discussion documents. Nonetheless, it is important for the health and efficacy of the WCC that its work should appear not only to belong together but positively to "hang together". Following the Vancouver assembly these questions crystallized into a discussion within the WCC of a "vital and coherent theology". Three leading theologians closely connected with the Council's work – José Míguez Bonino, an Argentinian Methodist; Paulos Mar Gregorios, Syrian Orthodox metropolitan; and M.M. Thomas, Mar Thoma Church, the latter two from India – gave leadership in this. Papers were published, and there was a day of discussion in the executive committee.

The major emphasis at that time was "justice, peace and the integrity of creation" (JPIC). This illustrated alike the promise, the problem and the necessity of trying to "do theology ecumenically". The Vancouver assembly had spoken of this study of JPIC as a "conciliar process", reopening the old debate about who speaks for the church and how.

The theological section of the preparatory document for the concluding meeting of the study, the world convocation held in Seoul, South Korea, in 1990, was criticized by many participants in that meeting, some finding it too difficult, others too abstract and yet others too "global" or too "Northern" in its perceptions – although much care had been taken to have it drafted by a group whose members came from all the main "wings" of the Council, and to have it revised twice to take account of comments by churches, action groups and interested individuals all over the world.

Justice, peace and the integrity of creation (JPIC) was a major WCC programmatic emphasis during the Vancouver-Canberra period. The first stage in the "conciliar process of mutual commitment (covenant)" to JPIC culminated with a world convocation in Seoul, Korea, in March 1990

From this debate, it became clear that the call for "coherence" did not mean there is or can be one single, normative ecumenical theology. The WCC may sometimes look like a great monolith, always saying more or less the same thing(s). For sure, there have been and may be again periods when a particular outlook gains such dominance within the council that it appears to play a normative role. Yet, the constitution and the history both rule out any such role. The whole point of a World Council of Churches is to keep the discussions open to all sides, to enable people of different backgrounds and expectations to listen to each other and seek the common mind of the churches.

Konrad Raiser, the German theologian who became general secretary of the WCC in 1993, has traced the intellectual history of the Council through several stages:

1. The beginnings of the ecumenical movement owed much to the evangelical revival of the 19th century and its reaction to widespread indifference to the gospel. This was largely a non-intellectual, non-denominational theology.

2. In the mid-1920s Protestant liberalism was in the ascendancy. The Life and Work movement (which, despite its slogan that "doctrine divides, service unites", did a lot of

theologizing) was much influenced by the social gospel in the USA and elsewhere.

3. In the 1930s the radical critique of that liberalism associated with such theologians as Karl Barth, Emil Brunner and Reinhold Niebuhr insisted that true theology depends only on God's self-revelation in scripture, not on human culture, and became increasingly influential in the ecumenical movement.

4. Biblical theology – interpreting the Bible from the point of view that sees God's initiative in Jesus Christ as the centre of the history of salvation – dominated ecumenical theology in the early years of the WCC.

5. The 1960s saw the waning of the influence of any great, systematic thinkers such as Karl Barth or Paul Tillich, in favour of a prophetic rediscovery of the function of theology in and for the many different contexts of human life. There was a growing call positively to "contextualize", rooting theological work in the historical and cultural settings in which it was pursued.

That history led to the diversity of theologies within the ecumenical movement at the outset of the 21st century. Alongside continued attempts to formulate theology in the traditional ways of the various confessions, and efforts – in Faith and Order as elsewhere – to articulate "consensus theology" acceptable across traditional barriers, there are many "genitive" theologies (theology *of* the poor, *of* liberation) as well as "adjectival" or "regional" theologies (feminist, black, Asian, Pacific, Central European).

All these theologies seek to be contextual, since each arises within and for a given context. Their existence as fellow-participants within the one ecumenical movement is not itself a mark of incoherence; rather it reflects the movement's diversity and vitality. As José Míguez put it, the coherence needed in ecumenical theology is that of "a living, growing organism", not the "mechanical coherence of a smoothly running machine". But if there is to be life and growth, he went on, there must also be interaction, mutual accountability and mutual correction. It is not enough to acknowledge that all theologies are contextual.

Such mutual accountability, Míguez suggested, is needed in three areas: "we are all accountable to each other for the way we use and interpret the scriptures; for our theology's relation to the manifold tradition of the church; and for the interpretation of reality implicit or explicit in our theological formulations."

Gregorios pointed in a similar direction in suggesting three conditions for an ecumenical theology to be both vital and coherent: "rootedness in the mind of the church as community of the Spirit as it has existed for 2000 years; full awareness of the main lines of political-economic, scientific-technological, social-cultural and philosophical-intellectual perceptions and discoveries in the contemporary world; and acquaintance with the suffering and experience of all the exploited and the oppressed, coupled with the compassion of Christ and a passion for justice, peace and the integrity of creation".

* * *

Thinking together in faith – theological reflection in the many ongoing dialogues with the Tradition – will surely continue to play a central role in the ecumenical movement. The calling of the WCC is to serve the whole fellowship of Christian churches, in and for their service to the whole of humanity and care for all life on the planet. If the Council is to be true to its heritage, it will always seek to hold together *both* Tradition and contemporary needs with serious and sustained intellectual work.

6. Does the WCC Really Matter?

This question has probably arisen several times during the reading of the previous chapters.

Who decides?

The key question is: "really matter" for whom? Who can take the decisions that flow from such an evaluation? Different discussions will be needed here. For instance, how much does the Council matter to Christians and the churches which are its members? How much does it matter to the world at large?

Within which context?

Second, one cannot but take note of the shifting contexts within which any such evaluation has to be made. Over the first fifty years of the Council's existence there have constantly been two broad flows of change in the wider context that affect its self-understanding and work.

1. Changing patterns of awareness and expectation for the world as a whole

The ending of international idealism

In the later 1940s memories of the second world war contrasted with hopes for a better world and gave impetus to the creation of international organizations such as the United Nations and the World Council of Churches, as well as countless efforts at more local levels.

To be sure, the hopes expressed by the delegates at the WCC Amsterdam assembly in 1948 were more tempered and realistic than the optimism just after the first world war. But the Amsterdam debates had their blind spots too. To stay with the host country, alongside the inspiring story of how the German pastor Martin Niemöller had been warmly received in the Dutch capital within three years of its liberation from German occupation, there is the recognition – with hindsight – that the assembly apparently gave no attention to the struggle, already long begun, of the Indonesian people for liberation from the Dutch.

Nonetheless, there was a period in the early days of the Council when international affairs could draw on a significant degree of idealism within the churches. People hoped that life would become better, if not for all humanity, at least for significant sections who had had difficult times in earlier generations. Looking back, this period does not seem to have lasted long.

Establishment of the two German states in 1948 and the crisis over Berlin in the winter of 1948-49 marked the consolidation of Europe into two mutually hostile camps, trapped into a hostility that was in later years to involve much of the rest of the world.

An event of special significance in the life of the World Council of Churches was the outbreak of war in Korea in 1950. A statement from the central committee which supported the action of the United Nations led to the resignation of the Chinese theologian T.C. Chao who had been made one of the Council's six presidents at the Amsterdam assembly, and was to prove a lastingly divisive sign of the "one-sidedness" of the Council for critics in the communist world.

The ending of post-colonial idealism

The granting of independence to India in 1947 is often taken as the beginning of the "coming of age" of the previously colonized peoples of the South.

Over the fifty years between Indian independence and the freeing of Nelson Mandela in 1989, the moment when South Africa could at last see its future lie with the rest of the South rather than primarily with the North, each newly independent country and each region of newly independent peoples had its time of fresh hopes and visions.

All too often, however, these moments were dismayingly brief. Just as the high hopes of 1945 were swept away within three years, so in Asia and Africa the internal conflicts, the struggles for economic autonomy, the influence of the rival great powers from the North, all soon swept away any innocence in their idealism.

Here, too, one moment in the history of the WCC shows how soon idealistic hopes of a "new day" between the formerly colonized and formerly colonizing nations had to give way to a sober, realistic and at times even confrontational atmosphere. In this case the "moment" came in 1966 at the Church and Society conference held in the new WCC headquarters in Geneva on "Christians in the Technical and Social Revolutions of Our Time". A conference with a majority of lay delegates and with the numbers from the third world slightly out-numbering those from the West was able to speak straight about, for instance, the economic dangers of a new Western imperialism or about the need for the churches in the richer nations to free themselves from the dominant attitudes to race or poverty in their countries.

The ending of the cold war

Any idealism at the end of the second world war regarding Marxism as a governing philosophy, or about the communist system, was an early casualty of Stalinism in those nations directly affected, and in face of the evidence leaking out from them could hardly last much longer in the rest of the world. All the same, a wave of new hope swept through the countries of Central and Eastern Europe as the Gorbachev reforms began to bite in the Soviet Union and sharpened into action in 1989 with the refusal of Hungarian border guards to prevent young people from the German Democratic Republic crossing their border into Austria and the ensuing collapse in one country after another of the communist parties and governments.

Here the WCC had been closely involved, in one way or another, throughout the forty years of cold war. Already at the founding assembly the Council's critique of both capitalism and communism had aroused the antagonism of media and governments on both sides. Moreover a growing number of third-world voices had from then on insisted that the division between the two blocs was really an inner-Western issue, and that the US-Soviet rivalry usually worked in the rest of the world against the interests of the "client" countries for whose support those blocs were competing.

Particularly after Orthodox churches from the Soviet Union and three other Eastern European countries were allowed to join the Council in 1961, the WCC was one of the few international organizations in which a measure of genuine fellowship across cold-war barriers could be maintained. But not without strains! The Council's action in regard to the Korean war (1950), then to the uprisings in Hungary (1956) and Czechoslovakia (1968), to the Vietnam war of the 1960s and to the Soviet invasion of Afghanistan in the 1980s all strained relationships to near-breaking points, though of course in ways that were interpreted differently by people of different view-points. For most of the WCC's existence until the 1990s the cold war was one of the dominant concerns, affecting many of the Council's actions in ways that could never be approved by all sections of its constituency.

Churches in Central and Eastern Europe all along faced severe restrictions. Protecting the narrow space in which they could operate and keeping alive the possibility of at least some participation in international meetings depended on staying in favour with atheistic governments. The WCC found it hard to say anything publicly about those governments which would not lead to harm for the member churches. But this led to charges of "selectivity" or "anti-Westernism" in some Western quarters.

When Mikhail Gorbachev and Ronald Reagan met in Geneva in November 1985, church leaders from the two countries came to Geneva, too, to pray for the success of the conversations. From then on, the churches played key roles in the loosening up of attitudes on both sides of the iron curtain.

Yet, the difficulties of moving into better forms of society proved almost everywhere to be far greater than was anticipated in those heady days of 1989-90.

The Soviet Union rapidly broke up into separate nations, some of them grouped into a Commonwealth of Independent

On the occasion of the Reagan-Gorbachev summit meeting in Geneva in 1985, religious leaders from the Soviet Union and the USA came together to pray for peace in Geneva's St Pierre cathedral. From left to right: Henry Babel (Switzerland), Bishop Longin (Russian Orthodox Church), Arie Brouwer (general secretary of the NCCCUSA), Metropolitan Filaret of Minsk and Byelorussia, Robert Neff and Rena Yocom (vice presidents of the NCCCUSA), Alexei Bichkov (general secretary of the Union of Evangelical Christian Baptists of the USSR), Asoghik Aristakesian (Armenian Orthodox Church)

States. Each of the Eastern European nations, from Estonia in the North to Bulgaria and Albania in the South seized the chance to re-shape itself, partly by its own long-repressed national traditions, partly by measures which it hoped would soon produce a Western-style economy. Some have been accepted into membership in NATO and look forward to the same in the European Union, while others – hardly less eager for those badges of a new maturity – have been compelled to wait. The former Yugoslavia crumbled still more tragically and messily into what began as five separate entities but may end up as more...

Meanwhile, other parts of the post-war communist "empire" have developed in their no less distinctive ways. Cuba has struggled to remain faithful to the vision of Fidel Castro, while China has proclaimed itself to be pursuing a socialism with a Chinese face that to many, inside no less than outside, looks amazingly like an opportunistic unloosing of the Chinese gifts for entrepreneurial innovation under an increasingly wobbly "party" of self-selecting leaders. The internal power-struggles of Cambodia contrast with the newly re-united Vietnam, while the world largely forgets about Laos. North Korea has become the focus of much attention, whether for its famine or its missiles, leading to talk of reunion there too.

In virtually every case, any "idealism" of the first stage has given way to a more sober and realistic appreciation of the difficulties to be faced.

Within these nations the situations of the churches, their expectations and initiatives, are every bit as different, as full of internal struggles and of often exaggerated and frustrated hopes of rescue from outside, as those of the new governments. Some look to the World Council of Churches for new versions of the fellowship and support it tried to give them in the communist period. Others – most notably the Russian Orthodox Church – prefer to trust in their own resources and traditions.

The Council continues to care for these as for other churches, while often hardly knowing how best to give reality to that care. An initial response from the central committee in March 1990 welcomed the new liberties and democratic processes while drawing attention to three dangers: uncritical acceptance of free-market capitalism as a solution to their economic malaise; a "Euro-centric" attitude ignoring poverty and oppression in the rest of the world; and the potential for conflict created by rising ethnic and national consciousness.

At the same time, the global situation, with the USA as the only super-power, free to impose its economic, military and cultural hegemony on all other parts of the world, does not promise lasting peace or prosperity for all. East Asia is becoming hardly less than a second super-power in waiting. Many voices continue to call for some sort of global governance, yet the United Nations has so far proved at best a weak model of anything that could reach that far.

Such a situation can be seen as even more clearly calling for a World Council of Churches, as for world organs of non-

Christian religions, striving to identify the paths of truth and health worth following, and to encourage leadership by Christians and others in many different places and spheres of concern. Yet this points to a Council that its member churches will need to give greater support.

2. Changing patterns of atmosphere and expectation in regard to religion

Over these more than fifty years two different – though not necessarily contradictory – characterizations have been much used as a convenient shorthand about the religious scene. Some, particularly in the North, have emphasized that the late 20th century has been *an age of rampant secularization*; others, more often in the South, point to the evidence for *an unprecedented surge in religious beliefs and emotions*. Both sets of evidence affect the life and work of the WCC.

An age of irreversible secularization?

Already the words used in responding to this question are far from clear.

• The term "secular", as an adjective, is usually seen as objectively descriptive: pointing to a system or institution in which no attention is given, or allowed to be given, to matters of religion. The constitution of the new India in 1947, for instance, insists that India shall be a secular state, in that all persons will be treated equally, without regard to their religion, and in that political parties and other institutions of the state would be formed within that provision by and for people of any religious faith or of none.

Such situations are generally welcomed by Christians where they are in a minority, and are felt to accord with what the ecumenical movement has taught about religious freedom. The history of Europe and North America, where Christians have been in the majority, are however full of instances where in one way or another "religious preference" continues to play a significant part in society, even in politics. It is far from true to suggest that Christians are invariably in favour of a secular state.

Moreover, the use of a word in a document is hardly a guarantee against developments that substantially alter the situation. Already in India the growing weight of opinion and emotion in the majority Hindu community has led to election of a Hindu party to govern with priorities that favour causes weighted towards Hindus, even exclusively advantaging them over others. Pakistan, a state that came into existence because of its Muslim majority, but promises to uphold "religious freedom", proves to be seriously in violation of key elements of what the United Nations affirms about religious liberty.

• Another area of debate circles round the appropriate line between the "religious" and the "secular" in various spheres of human life. Take marriage, for instance. Almost every people and culture has its characteristic patterns and practices in the sphere of man-woman relationships, sexual behaviour and expectations, the institution of marriage and the expectations concerning widowhood, separation and divorce that accompany it. Moreover many of these patterns are felt to belong in some essential way to the main religious tradition of that people, with a number of variants or exceptions for other religious traditions or communities. But exactly what the link between the "religion" and the "cultural practice" consists of often proves difficult to pinpoint.

Is it against true Christian obedience for a married couple to divorce? Some churches say "yes", others "no". While the Roman Catholic Church has historically taken a strong line against divorce, it has developed the practice of matrimonial courts testing whether the marriage was a true one to start with, and nowadays is prepared to recognize that many marriages apparently were not, so that they may be dissolved. Where in this is "culture", where "religion", and just where does the line run?

Another example arises with the meaning of major social festivals. In majority-Christian countries, Christmas and Easter have long been key points in national and social life. Yet with modern changes many Christians feel that the economic concerns of shopkeepers selling Christmas presents, as of travel agents offering enticing holidays, have so come to dominate these festivals that the original "religious" meaning has been overshadowed. It is often said that these festivals have become unduly "secularized". Others will however say that originally both festivals developed in relation to earlier, in no way "Christian" social observances, Christmas to do with the sun at mid-winter and Easter to do with the rebirth of vegetation in spring. Were they not "secular" before they became "Christian"?

• The same term "secularization" has often been used in debates among Christian missionaries about the appropriate attitudes they should take to customs and festivals of the people they have come to serve. As some members of this people come to believe in Jesus, should they continue to follow the practices of their people – in pouring libations as an act of prayer, or in modes of dress – or adopt some variant of the practice of the missionaries? (Those new Christians often had their own opinions, too, of course!) In some cases it was felt appropriate to see the indigenous custom as not necessarily belonging to the previous "religion" of the people, and therefore as remaining appropriate; in others a strict line was drawn between the way of life of Christians and that of others which allowed relatively little to be shared across it.

• In a more general sense the term "secularization" is used to describe the replacement of a world-view that appeals to supernatural, usually religious, explanations for events and realities by explanations in secular terms. This process is usually seen as more or less inevitable and irreversible.

Among Christians this development since the Enlightenment of the 18th century has often been seen as positive. Not only were many of the pioneers of modern Western science, like Isaac Newton, devout Christians. A secular approach to, say, epidemics of flu as something caused by known micro-organisms whose spread can be prevented will relieve human suffering far better than a religious acceptance of the plague as a divine judgment.

Yet in recent debates, especially as it has become possible to take a many-sided view of the relationships between the previously dominant West and the cultures of the formerly colonial peoples, thinking within the ecumenical movement has become far more chastened about the potential of the secular. We have come to recognize just how often modern science and technology have grown out of a certain West-centred world-view and been made to serve the interests of the West. Developments in genetics, discussed in the report on bio-technology mentioned on p.150 above raise profound theological questions by their very secularity:

> In many respects, the scientific perspectives undergirding bio-technology function according to a mechanistic world-view where living organisms are referred to as "self-replicating molecular machines" that can be snipped, programmed, cloned, designed, replicated and manipulated at will. Life is thus objectified and can be reduced to assemblages of molecules designed for purely utilitarian and instrumental ends... The life of the creation is reduced to the status of "resources" to be mastered, efficiently used, engineered and – when no longer profitable – discarded.

A growing number of people in many different cultures, by no means only Christians, are rejecting this Western secularism which views the entire world – history, economics and politics quite as much as science itself – as though God and anything beyond human understanding were unnecessary for an adequate understanding of reality.

• Along with this intellectual debate, there is no less worry and concern about the effect of an unchallenged dominance of typical Western, "secularized" attitudes on the moral sense and sensibility of the younger generations now growing up. Many examples can be found of this. One with obvious consequences for the work of the WCC is the apparent erosion of a sense of solidarity with those who are poor or deprived which accompanies the growth of materialism in consumer societies. The willingness to shrug one's shoulders at the pictures of hunger, disease and suffering in other parts of the world that fill the TV screens and the newspapers of the West, often called "compassion fatigue", has profound consequences for any organization seeking to raise funds and to recruit people ready to devote time and skills to help those in need. The domination of a secular outlook (let alone one secularized by unrecognised socio-economic forces) that gives priority to the individual over the social, and to financial outcomes over human relationships, is better seen as a threat to the Christian view of life.

• That leads into the question of the reason for the apparent loss of religious, specifically of Christian, faith in large parts of the West. Here too the word "secularization" is often used for a far-reaching, long-range, and largely inexplicable socio-cultural development with which the worldwide Christian family has yet to come to terms. But there is no denying the decline in active participation in most of the older churches of Europe and North America.

Two examples of this come from the experience of the WCC. The first has to do with the role of the press. To cover the third WCC assembly in New Delhi in 1961 the largest circulation US newsweekly sent a team of journalists, including its editor-in-chief, and featured a portrait of the WCC general secretary on the cover of that week's issue. Yet by the time of the sixth assembly in Vancouver 1983 the same periodical gave it no more than a single page, discussing only one topic on the Assembly's agenda – its statement on Soviet intervention in Afghanistan.

The second is in the decline in financial support that the WCC receives from its member churches in the prosperous Western countries. In the early years there were significant gifts from wealthy donors in the USA, alongside a high level of giving from the US member churches. In the 1960s these began to fall off. Their place in the Council's finances was taken by the churches in Western Germany, benefiting very greatly from a unique system of church tax calculated as a percentage of income tax. But in the 1990s, the German churches found themselves less able to maintain earlier commitments.

Are these examples due to "secularization", or to something more closely related to what is counted as acceptable power or influence in the leading circles of a given nation?

There is much more that can and needs to be explored in this debate. One thing, however, important for the WCC, is clear: whereas in the early years of the WCC many churches of the South and in the poorer areas of the North looked to the Council for help with their material and financial needs, the churches of the West now no less urgently need the solidarity and support of the churches in other cultural and political situations for their task of witness among their largely indifferent fellow-citizens.

From one point of view, more positive developments pose even sharper challenges to the ecumenical movement.

A far-reaching revival in the other traditional world faiths

In the mid-1950s, as former colonies in Asia gained their independence, a renascence in their historic faiths – Buddhism, Hinduism and Islam – was recognized as an important factor in the nation-building they had begun and would now swiftly develop. This has indeed happened, if with many different accents and results in different contexts and at the different stages of the paths these nations have taken.

Christians, especially during the era of Western colonial dominance, had too often dismissed these other world religions as irrelevant, if not primitive or pagan. Few people in the West had any first-hand acquaintance with devout people of other faiths, and among the missionaries who did many warned their supporters back home (not least because it was good for money-raising!) that other faiths were the enemies of Christianity.

Yet in the latter part of the 20th century this mood changed, partly because of the impression made by such figures as Mahatma Gandhi and Martin Buber, partly because of the growing number of adherents of the other faiths coming to the West as students, statesmen and evangelists, partly because of the growing awareness that Christianity was not going to supplant those faiths in their homelands.

So the witness of many missionaries about justice, courtesy and love as marks of the appropriate Christian attitude to neighbours of a different faith gradually made its way into the wider Christian community. That witness had played a role already at the Edinburgh world mission conference in 1910, whose efforts in this field – neglected in face of other urgent concerns for most of the inter-war period – were taken up anew in the 1960s when the WCC began to take a serious interest in interfaith dialogue.

Meanwhile the need for more extensive and fair-minded awareness of the range of religious traditions at work in today's world has continued to grow, again partly because of the influence of leading figures – the Dalai Lama for one – partly because so many of the conflicts around the world involve some sort of difference or division in religious allegiance (Sri Lanka, Lebanon, Palestine/Israel, Northern Ireland, Kosovo/Serbia, etc.), and not least because of the growing number of people of different faiths living in virtually all the more developed countries. In North America and Western Europe interfaith activities have come to enjoy an enthusiasm and commitment on the part of many Christians who regard interchurch activities as of much lesser value.

The rise of "new religious movements"

At the same time recent years have witnessed a rise of many new religious movements (some in fact new versions of an older tradition). The Unification Church of Sun Myung Moon and the International Society of Krishna Consciousness (known as the Hare Krishna) are hardly cousins to each other, still less friends. Two points that are often seen as common are their priority on witnessing to young people, and their claim to offer a synthesis or syncretism of two or more of the historic faiths that makes them even more adequate than any single tradition.

The number and diversity of such New Religious Movements (NRMs) make it impossible to develop any single response from within the Christian community. Some make a considerable impact, others much less. Some of them raise issues of religious freedom in a particularly difficult form. In some countries they have proved to be a force for destabilizing society, in others they appear at times to be providing an

African Instituted Churches have grown phenomenally over recent decades and have a strong worship life. Here, the Jerusalem Church of Christ, Kenya Panos Pictures

ideological home for the interests of a repressive political or military regime. Christian churches have on the whole been more wary of friendly dialogue with adherents of NRMs than with historic world religions, fearful that the NRM may use dialogue as a platform to propagate anti-Christian views or as a means of gaining recognition and legitimacy.

The rise of "new" Christian churches

The 20th century saw the rise of thousands of African Instituted Churches (AICs) with millions of members. Each has its own leader(s), teachings, social/linguistic base, history, etc. within the mosaic of African peoples and cultures. Those attracting large numbers of members included the Church of Jesus Christ on Earth by the Prophet Simon Kimbangu (principally in the formerly Belgian Congo) and the Zion Christian Church of Engenas Lekganyane (principally in South Africa). Many others are smaller and less well organized.

The diversities among them include different levels of awareness of their standing in the tradition of historic Christianity. Use of the term "church" suggests a sense of community with the "historic-mission" churches, but in practice that cannot always be relied on. Any involvement from among them with the WCC has been relatively slow, though this has now moved ahead in some places. The Kimbanguists of Congo/Zaire were accepted into Council membership in 1969, and have been followed by a few of the others.

A comparable movement has been proceeding in Latin America. Here the key term used is "Pentecostalism" – though in many cases the link with the historic Pentecostal denominations is tenuous. As in Africa, what is most important is that this is a form of religious/Christian faith and practice that people have found/discovered/developed themselves, not a faith taken over from some "other" or "outsider". Both the Roman Catholic Church introduced into this continent by the Spanish and Portuguese invaders five hundred years ago, and the more recent arrival of Protestant Christianity, largely through communities of Europeans coming to settle for the sake of their own future, have failed to touch large numbers of Latin Americans. Yet with the marginalization (often virtually the genocide) of almost all the indigenous peoples, little continuity is possible with the traditional religions of the continent. So people have been left on their own to discover a faith that can give meaning and purpose to lives much disturbed by modern urban and economic developments.

As in Africa, the few beginnings of contacts between these Pentecostal churches and the ecumenical movement, let alone the WCC, have had little wider effect. Two Chilean Pentecostal churches were accepted into WCC membership in the 1960s, joined later by a third. But a Brazilian Pentecostal church which joined in the 1970s withdrew not many years later. Since the Harare assembly, however, a more sustained form of contact between these churches and the WCC has been initiated.

A third large constituency of Christians at present almost entirely outside the ecumenical movement is to be found in China. Here the links with foreign missionaries stretch far back – to the year 635 when the Persian monk Aloben, of what we now know as the (Nestorian) Church of the East, arrived at the capital, Chang'An (now Xi'an) of the Tang Emperor Tai Zong, and was given permission to build a monastery and preach this new faith.

Yet here too the long history of foreign missions had hardly won what looked like major success, and was thought to have been largely washed out by the communist victory in 1949 and its aftermath.

But as Deng Xiao Ping led China into a new phase after the death of Mao in 1976, religious freedom was re-instituted and some of the old churches started to re-open in 1980. Since then, there has been a growing flood of new Christians appearing in almost every part of that enormous country. The Chinese government at the outset of the 21st century spoke of some 10 million Protestants and 8 million Catholics. The true figures are probably much greater.

Two very different spiritual movements have been going on within China. On the one hand a surge of religious emotion and new belief has taken Christian (more often Protestant but not seldom Catholic) form in new churches of the "little" people of the cities and, still more, the rural areas. These have felt in practice betrayed and abandoned, literally and spiritually, by all the earlier teachers and leaders, whether political or religious, in the maelstrom of the Cultural Revolution and since.

Starting later, and with much smaller numbers involved, there has been a still more astonishing surge of religious interest in the universities. Since 1949 not one has had any sort of theological faculty, yet by 1999 most of these had at least one teacher giving regular lectures in religious studies (usually in practice about Christianity), with many having opened some sort of institute for research and publication in this field, in partnership with the world religions section of the Chinese academy for social sciences. These "culture Christians" have not often had much, if any, contact with the churches, still less with Christian intellectuals of their own level of academic achievement (of whom there are in the churches very few). Yet, again out of the vacuum in contemporary China of any serious ideological or religious thinking, these academics, now in their hundreds, maybe thousands, have read and thought their way into convictions about the Christian faith as a key to the kind of future they can believe in.

The "historic-mission" churches in Africa, too, are experiencing growth in many areas, often areas such as Northern Nigeria where until the mid-20th century there were very few Christians at all. In Europe, particularly but not only in France, there has been a surge in Christian conviction among the Romanies/Gypsies in the later 20th century.

These new surges in religious faith point to major demands on those who give leadership to the ecumenical movement. The Council is seeking to discover paths of fellowship, understanding and support involving all Christians, "new" no less than "old", and of open, constructive relationships with other religions.

So, does the World Council of Churches really matter?

Against the background of these changes, what needs to be said in response to the question with which this chapter began?

The WCC exists because of the divisions among the churches. It exists to help them overcome and reconcile those divisions. So the realities of change, of diversities, of tensions, of disagreements are built into its very nature.

At the same time, as we have seen, the WCC neither has nor seeks any authority itself to function as the healer of these divisions. The 1950 Toronto Statement calls the WCC "a new and unprecedented approach to the problem of interchurch relationships", and specifies that the WCC must never claim that it has, let alone embodies, *the one and only* answer to that problem. The Council is no more than one of the instruments God may use, even if it is committed to the belief that the ecumenical movement is what the Holy Spirit has called into being for this purpose. So the question of success or failure for the WCC can never be measured simply by what proportion of existing churches have become its members or how many united churches have come into being.

For any careful evaluation of a religious institution or process, it makes a great deal of difference whether one is looking at the evidence "from inside" or "from outside".

Looking from inside – an impressive record?

From inside, as people whose churches have long been involved, let us consider the various images of the Council that we looked at in the first pages of this book.

• *The international relief agency:* In this regard the Council undoubtedly continues to matter greatly, both to those hit by emergencies, as to those whose continuing needs for development are great. Its working patterns have changed, so that it acts less today as the "grand centralizer" than as an enabling body, with the initiatives often now taken at levels much closer to local realities. Yet to pretend it is no longer useful would be unjust to the scale of continuing need in many parts of the world.

• *The broker of fresh ideas and approaches among the churches:* Here again, while the WCC makes no large claims about the extent to which its many study groups, consultations and conferences have influenced the churches, it has undoubtedly pursued its calling in this sphere with dogged persistence, leaving – as it must – the outcome to the care of the member churches.

• *The herald of good news to the poor:* Poverty and disease continues to dominate the lives of a huge proportion of the human family. Yet the WCC has continued to insist that priority be given not just to helping the poor but to partnership with the poor, and to re-shaping economic, political and social life so all can play their part.

• *The provider of opportunities for learning and for prayer:* The WCC's sponsorship of the annual Week of Prayer for Christian Unity, together with the Roman Catholic Church, remains a key piece of ecumenical service; its part in modelling fresh patterns for worship in its meetings over the last twenty years of the 20th century was one of its most hopeful and joyous contributions in the view of many participants. As for learning, while it is true that already by the 1970s any sense of it being "fashionable" within religious education in the richer part of the world to pay attention to the agenda of the ecumenical movement had passed, at least in some circles, most often in the poorer world that agenda does not disappear. The WCC continues, in its Ecumenical Institute at Bossey, in training courses held in the different regions, in its publications, and in virtually all its programmes, to encourage people to think and then act intelligently and together across the divisive boundaries.

• *The servant of peace and reconciliation:* Sometimes the WCC has served directly as a mediator and reconciler between hostile forces, as in regard to the war in the Sudan in the mid-1970s. At other times its service has been as prophet, persisting in the call to change of heart, as in regard to South Africa until 1989. At all times it has tried to serve the churches as herald of the centrality of work for peace in every context, whether that be of open hostility, as in the torn areas of, say, the Middle East, Sri Lanka or Northern Ireland, or – more often – in the contexts of grinding neglect and isolation – like Afghanistan, or Cambodia, or the Amazon, or the Marshall Islands.

• *The enabler of a sense of global citizenship:* With the WCC having arisen out of the work of missionaries, it has held open not just the possibility, rather the vocation of universal love and co-citizenship to all Christians. It has not been able to involve so very many individual persons in its programmes and meetings, but its existence has served as an encouragement to many different groups (young people, women, church leaders, etc, etc.) to seek out their opposite numbers in other churches, cultures and countries.

Looking from outside – fragility?

From outside, what probably strikes most strongly is an awareness of the fragility of the WCC.

At one level this fragility is a matter of *scarce resources*. To work at the range of tasks the member churches want done, and to meet the many expectations its history and experience have aroused, the WCC has far from enough money and personnel. The Council depends almost entirely for money on churches in Western Europe and North America which are mostly wrestling with financial difficulties themselves.

In earlier periods the member churches in the richer countries have been generous in providing the resources, including staff salaries and provision for pensions, the Council has needed. As well as the shrinkage in church membership in these areas, many of these churches have become involved in a range of interchurch bodies, each of which makes similar demands, i.e. local, national, regional and confessional fellowships which have their own programmes and meetings and staff, all of which depend on contributions from the same pool of churches. At the same time the churches in the poorer countries, many of them with infinitely less by way of transferable money to spend, continue to call for their Council to pursue agenda points of importance to them. The proportion of member churches who do not pay anything into the Council's budget remains uncomfortably high.

Moreover even the money that is made available carries other limitations. Most churches pay in their national currencies. So the value to the WCC is vulnerable to rises and falls in exchange rates. The Council has discussed whether Geneva is the right place for it to be based, yet between the cost of moving and the value of being close to agencies of the United Nations, the decision has always been to soldier on in the hope that the Swiss franc will not go on proving so difficult.

At a different level, the WCC looks to the outsider surprisingly fragile in respect of the *constant criticism* that it receives from a number of quarters. This may be summarized under four headings: political, theological, ecclesiological and institutional.

1. Again and again it is said that the WCC has subordinated its concern for church unity to political matters that should be left to other people. The fact that this charge has been made from the beginning of the Council's life may indicate that it points to deep differences in understanding of Christian obedience.

In the 1970s and 1980s, critics charged that WCC public statements, not least those concerning apartheid in South Africa and the need to overcome racism, exhibited "selective indignation" and a "left-ward tilt". Some critics were especially strident in regard to the Programme to Combat Racism, suggesting that money from church members was given to Marxist guerrillas.

Yet criticism of the WCC on political grounds has not been only Western. The *People's Daily* from Beijing, saw the 1961 integration of the International Missionary Council into the WCC as a "new strategy of American imperialist missionary enterprise". Soviet media attacked the WCC's stand on human rights at the fifth assembly of 1975. In the 1980s Brazilian landowners described WCC support for the land rights of indigenous people there as a conspiracy with US interests to violate the country's sovereignty. In the tangle of Middle Eastern politics, the WCC has been attacked from all sides at different times, sometimes blamed for activities of Christian groups with which it has no connection.

2. Theological criticisms of the WCC vary no less than the political according to who is making them and in which context. One common type is the objection that the Council over-emphasizes one side or another of the inevitable tension between "doctrinal" and "social" concerns.

More serious are the accusations that the WCC neglects mission and evangelism. The statement adopted by the central committee in 1982 called *Mission and Evangelism: An Ecumenical Affirmation* has not stilled objections. Interfaith dialogue too spurs many to protest about the sidelining of evangelism.

Some criticize the WCC for a view of human nature that is too optimistic, a view of sin that focuses too much on social structures, not enough on personal evil, and too uncritical a faith in human potential for bringing in the kingdom of God.

So also some people in the Reformed tradition have seen in WCC texts such as that on *Baptism, Eucharist and Ministry* a "catholicizing" tendency which they say subordinates the word to the sacraments or downplays the ministry of all believers. Orthodox churches charge that the WCC overemphasizes Protestant concerns.

3. The nature of the WCC as a fellowship of nationally organized churches has been criticized by some in the "believers' church" tradition, who insist that the body of Christ can only become visible "from below", as a local congregation gathers around word and sacrament. The pattern of national churches, some representatives of the "historic peace churches" have argued, explains why the WCC never takes a theologically consistent stand against war.

Others say that the WCC Basis does not specify enough of the non-negotiable elements of the Christian faith, or object that though every member church of the Council has to "express agreement" with the Basis, there is no way of verifying their assent. This is the root of the "separatist" argument that affiliation with the WCC is a scripturally prohibited alliance with unbelievers. Still others argue that the WCC is too "church-oriented" and does not do sufficient justice to the contribution of more informal or local Christian communities and movements.

4. As the ecumenical movement has evolved, some say, its institutionalization has created a bureaucratic way of working that is rigid, unimaginative, preoccupied with self-preservation. Others point out that in face of so many human needs the WCC too often opens up new programmes before the older ones have had a real chance to show their worth, making the whole Council an over-complicated organization lacking in coordination.

WCC ethical positions on current issues are sometimes criticized as idealistic or ignorant of the technical complexities of the topics they address. Many unfavourable comments about its way of working are voiced, and critics point to the expense of numerous international conferences producing long documents that appeal to a limited readership.

A brief response to its critics

As an institution devoted to healing conflicts, the WCC must also be a forum for bringing these disagreements into the open. Moreover, as an international body, its approach to any local situation or issue will likely be unsatisfying to those who live in that context. It may become evident that many criticisms of the WCC are rooted in different emphases rather than actual disagreement.

Even when it hurts, criticism is nevertheless to be welcomed. It can identify and help correct blind spots, challenging what can easily become set myths and clichés among insiders. The health of any institution with highly committed people always needs stringent comment, since their dedication to its causes can lead them to lose perspective.

For whatever may or may not deserve to be said about it, there should be no claim that the WCC is anything else than one more human institution among others, subject to all the familiar failings and weaknesses. Neither the nobility of its vocation, nor the breadth of participation in its decision-making exempt it from error or lapses in respect of balance or wisdom.

But many of the critiques of the WCC, indeed most of the most widely publicized of them, are less of the constructive variety than ideologically based objections which fail to stand up when looked at from outside the particular mind-set that they express. They trade on stereotypes reinforced by deliberate campaigns to misrepresent and discredit the Council.

Yes, it matters, and for quite identifiable reasons

1. The first reason why the WCC continues to matter, after all the internal debates, after all the outside critiques, is that disunity is dangerous. In the words of a Northern Irish speaker to the fifth assembly of 1975, "Divided churches cost lives." Disunity between churches cannot but produce ignorance and fear. Dividedness as a matter of fact can easily slide over into divisiveness as a matter of attitude. Some may argue that today, among Christians at least, religious wars are a thing of the past; yet there are still conflicts in some parts of the world which would seem an eloquent and apparently still unresolvable witness that this is no universal truth.

In other cases – Kashmir, Sri Lanka or the Holy Land – a look at ethnic backgrounds, pattern of land ownership and overall economic history will show that the killing has little to do with religious beliefs. Even there, however, the fact that the communities at war with each other can call upon different religious traditions is likely to intensify hostilities.

Unless religious faith can operate as a force for understanding and reconciliation it will inevitably at times of stress be used to fan the flames of hatred. Even where members of different Christian churches are not shooting at each other, their reciprocal anathemas or mutual charges of heresy create an image that is a counter-witness to what any of them may be trying to say about the gospel, and deprive the wider society of a force that could, under other circumstances, work for the realization of "one human family in justice and peace".

So the fellowship of different churches in councils like the WCC is at one and the same time a challenge to the stereotypes, as to any sense of superiority and self-suffi-

Morning worship at the Harare assembly (1998)   WCC/Chris Black

ciency, that create divisions, and a witness to the goal of reconciliation.

2. The WCC is a unique instrument for disclosing the interplay of the local and the global. It is at the local level that any vision of church unity must take root, yet the centrality of the local parish or congregation must never become parochialism. Local churches are all called to fulfil their "common calling", not just to live by themselves. The body of Christ is intrinsically a universal reality.

Nowhere is as wide a range of local Christian voices heard as in the WCC; nowhere can the global dimensions of major contemporary issues be addressed as completely. Their participation in the WCC helps all churches see their political, social and economic contexts as interconnected with those of fellow-Christians in far-away places. Yet this same fact forbids any of us to treat realities such as "the international debt crisis", or "racism", or "nuclear testing", or "drug abuse" as mere "issues" to be looked at sometime by someone else. They are urgent cries from our neighbours, giving a human face to what can otherwise be negligible abstractions.

3. "Glory be to God for dappled things!" wrote the poet Gerard Manley Hopkins. The colourful diversity of the worldwide Christian family is itself something to be celebrated. In few arenas is this as evident as within the World Council of Churches. Countless people have testified to the inspiration they have drawn from joining in a worship service at a WCC conference; even such a simple thing as sharing in a congregation where the Lord's prayer is said simultaneously in twenty or thirty languages is overwhelmingly joyful to those who experience it for the first time.

Among Christians, cultural diversities, which are by no means the same as disagreements, are a much-needed corrective to any tendency to absolutize our own particular forms of being Christian, and so to that dangerously common form of calling attention more to ourselves than to the purposes of God.

4. Even if it is difficult to draw direct lines of cause-and-effect between things the WCC says or does and subsequent

events in world history, it remains true that besides church unity the Council has been instrumental in alleviating the misery of millions, offering hope to people in despair, interceding on behalf of victims of human rights violations, and reconciling warring parties. In many situations, the church has proved more effective at delivering needed assistance than other organizations, and by pooling the churches' resources the WCC has greatly enhanced their effectiveness.

Visiting the 1998 WCC assembly in Harare, President Nelson Mandela said:

> To us in South and Southern Africa, and indeed the entire continent, the WCC has always been known as a champion of the oppressed and exploited... The vast majority of our people heard the name of the WCC with joy. It encouraged and inspired us... Above all you respected the judgment of the oppressed as to what were the most appropriate means for attaining their freedom... Thirty years ago you launched a programme that broke new ground and set directions for the future. You moved beyond the affirmation of the right to resist on the part of the oppressed, to the risk of active engagement in the struggle to end oppression. Today the WCC is called to show that same engagement in the new and more difficult struggle for development and the entrenchment of democracy. That is why I put aside everything else to come today and say, "Thank you".

5. The most basic reason for believing that the WCC matters is not however any of these relatively pragmatic ones, but the conviction that the vision of unity in Christ which drives the WCC is a biblical and theological imperative, not something that grows out of sentimental notions of harmony, or woolly ideas of tolerance.

It all grows out of Jesus' prayer recorded in John 17:21f. – "that they all may be one", not forgetting the words that follow, "as you, Father, are in me and I in you, may they also be in us, so that the world may believe that you have sent me". Jesus' words not only encourage us to work for the unity of the church, but set that unity in the framework of the relationship of believers to God.

Some will be quick to point out that the perfect oneness for which Jesus prayed is not to be expected this side of death, for the forces of sin and division will continue until the final consummation. Yet the WCC represents the enduring conviction, never entirely absent in church history but especially flowering in the 20th century, that neither the elusiveness of ultimate success nor the recognition of unity as God's gift, nor our achievement, exempts us from working for it.

In their message to the churches, delegates to the first assembly of the WCC said:

> It is not in human power to banish sin and death from the earth, to create the unity of the holy catholic church, to conquer the hosts of Satan. But it is within the power of God. He has given us at Easter the certainty that his purpose will be accomplished.
>
> But, by our acts of obedience and faith, we can on earth set up signs which point to the coming victory, till the day of that victory our lives are hid with Christ in God, and no earthly disillusion or distress or power of hell can separate us from him. As those who wait in confidence and joy for their deliverance, let us give ourselves to those tasks which lie to our hands, and so set up signs...

Setting up signs as "acts of obedience and faith" may sound like an over-modest aim for a global organization like the WCC. But the significance of the phrase should not be understated. In recent years the notion of the church as "sign" has gained renewed attention in the ecumenical movement. For the church to live as a sign means "showing forth Christ as he becomes alive in a particular situation", as a 1973 consultation said, putting no limits on what God may intend to do through us.

* * *

These chapters have shown that a portrait of the WCC can never be a finished one. When dramatic events shake the life of the world and the church, the WCC may act boldly and significantly, in what may look like radical new ways. For most of the time, however, no such *kairos* is evident. Yet the faithful, even unspectacular work of encouraging the churches to grow in unity, witness, service and renewal goes on, equipping them to face the next unexpected crisis.

Does the WCC really matter? Is the ecumenical movement really moving?

The questions remain; now will never be the time for final answers. Not everybody will think that the WCC really matters; not everybody will agree that despite the annoying hold-ups the ecumenical movement does move. So the WCC keeps on, in both word and deed, reminding the churches and all their members of the necessity, paradoxically, of both *patience* – the recognition that in unity in Christ as in mountain climbing, the nearer you get to the goal the slower the progress – and of the *holy impatience* with the status quo that started off the movement in the first place.

You may like to finish this chapter and book by praying with millions of others the closing prayer from the statement "Our Ecumenical Vision" used at Harare by the eighth assembly:

> God of unity, God of love,
> what we say with our lips, make strong in our hearts,
> what we affirm with our minds, make vivid in our lives.
> Send us your Spirit
> - to pray in us what we dare not pray,
> - to claim us beyond our own claims,
> - to bind us when we are tempted to go our own ways.
> Lead us forward.
> Lead us together.
> Lead us to do your will,
> the will of Jesus Christ, our Lord.
> Amen

Further Reading

Different readers with different backgrounds and experience in regard to the ecumenical movement will be looking for very different possibilities. These few pages try to point in several major directions without claiming to be comprehensive. Many of the books mentioned will refer to other useful texts. Access to these books is often a problem: the library of a university or of a national theological college/seminary should be able to help. The WCC is itself an active publisher: WCC Publications will send their current catalogue on request.

Basic reading

Both *Mission and Evangelism – An Ecumenical Affirmation* (1982) and *Baptism, Eucharist and Ministry* (1982) remain encouraging "consensus texts" in two vital areas of passionate division in the past. *Worshipping Ecumenically: Orders of Service from Global Meetings with Suggestions for Local Use* (1998), edited by Per Harling, and *With All God's People* (1989), edited by John Carden, are workbooks to enrich worship and prayer with important material from a great variety of Christian traditions and information about Christians throughout the world. *The Art of Forgiveness: Theological Reflections on Healing and Reconciliation* (1997) by Geiko Müller-Fahrenholz is a moving lead into one key feature, while *Living Letters: Report of Visits to the Churches during the Ecumenical Decade – Churches in Solidarity with Women* (1997) vividly portrays the increasingly important agenda brought forward by women in the churches. A subscription to the WCC's series of RISK books, four short studies per year on current priorities, is one way of keeping informed. Another, more frequent, source of news is the monthly *Ecumenical News International* (available in print or on e-mail – write to ENI at the address above).

For students and specialists

Look for the three large and comprehensive volumes of *History of the Ecumenical Movement*: vol. 1 – 1517-1948, edited by Stephen Neill and Ruth Rouse; vol. 2 – 1948-68, edited by H. Fey, these two also available in a single volume; vol. 3 – 1968-2000, edited by Norman Hjelm. Each contains detailed essays and comprehensive bibliographies. There is also the *Dictionary of the Ecumenical Movement* (2nd edition 2002) with over 600 entries, fully cross-referenced. *Together on the Way*, the official report of the latest WCC assembly, the eighth in Harare, Zimbabwe, in 1998, edited by Diane Kessler, is the essential text for policy, constitution, the list of member churches and current projects, etc.; easier to read will be an overall account of the assembly such as Martin Conway's *Journeying Together towards Jubilee*. The WCC's two quarterly journals, *The Ecumenical Review* and the *International Review of Mission*, contain a wide spread of articles, documents and book reviews on current questions. For an example of how ecumenical thinking can provoke unusually creative approaches, try Geiko Müller-Fahrenholz's *God's Spirit: Transforming a World in Crisis* (1995).

The history of the Council within the ecumenical movement

Two classic studies, each essential, are *The Genesis and Formation of the World Council of Churches* (1982) by W.A. Visser 't Hooft, the WCC's first general secretary, and *Ecumenical Foundations: A History of the International Missionary Council and Its 19th Century Background* (1952) by W.R. Hogg. *The Ecumenical Movement: An Anthology of Key Texts and Voices* (1998), edited by M. Kinnamon and B.E. Cope, is a useful sampling of documents, while *And So Set Up Signs* (1988) is a richly illustrated, popular account of the WCC's first forty years. For a scholarly study which excitingly overturns a widespread myth that has done much damage, see *Justice, Courtesy and Love: Theologians and Missionaries Encountering World Religions 1846-1914* (1995) by Kenneth Cracknell on the background to the Edinburgh 1910 world missionary conference's view of inter-religious contact and dialogue.

World mission and evangelism

New Directions in Mission and Evangelization (1992), edited by J. Scherer and S. Bevans, vol. 1 – Basic Statements, and vol. 2 – Theological Foundations, contain an invaluable selection of texts from all the major confessions and continents. *Called to One Hope: The Gospel in Diverse Cultures* (1998), edited by Christopher Duraisingh, is the official report of the tenth of the world mission conferences, now held by the WCC every ten years or so, since Edinburgh 1910. *Transforming Mission: Paradigm Shifts in Theology of Mission* (1991) by David Bosch is a tour de force by a single scholar, combining Bible studies, history and contemporary theological explorations. *The Isaiah Vision: An Ecumenical Strategy for Congregational Evangelism* (1992) by Raymond Fung is a short, deceptively simple but powerful tool.

Towards unity in faith and in order

Confessing the One Faith: An Ecumenical Explication of the Apostolic Faith (1999) is a bold workbook from the Faith and Order commission, helping Christians of all confessions to discover a real unity of faith in the Nicene-Constantinopolitan Creed of 381. *Ecclesiology and Ethics: Ecumenical Ethical Engagement, Moral Formation and the Nature of the Church* (1997), edited by Thomas Best and Martin Robra, contains three reports on how Christian unity interweaves with ethical and social obedience, along with essays exploring the wider dimensions. *On the Way to Fuller Koinonia* (1994), edited by Thomas Best and Günther Gassmann, is the official report of the latest world conference on Faith and Order. Much effort has been poured in recent years into work on relations between the Protestant member churches of the WCC and their sister Orthodox members, reflected in *Orthodox Visions of Ecumenism: Statements, Messages and Reports on the Ecumenical Movement 1902-1992* (1994), edited by Gennadios Limouris, which reproduces fifty important texts by Orthodox leaders and representatives from their participation in the ecumenical strivings of the 20th century. *Eucharist and*

Witness: Orthodox Perspectives on the Unity and Mission of the Church (1998), by Petros Vassiliadis, and *The Sense of Ecumenical Tradition* (1991), by Ion Bria, are two personal explorations in the same large area. In regard to relations with the Roman Catholic Church, from the enormous literature try *The Bishop of Rome* (1982) by J.-M.R. Tillard, the former Roman Catholic vice-chairman of the Faith and Order commission; *Better Together: Christian Partnership in a Hurt City* (1988) by D. Worlock and D. Sheppard, the Catholic and Anglican bishops of Liverpool, UK, an outstanding story from the local level; and *Barriers To Ecumenism: The Holy See and the World Council on Social Questions* (1983) by T.S. Derr, an important warning that good relations cannot be taken for granted. *Truth and Community: Diversity and its Limits in the Ecumenical Movement* (1988) is a key study of one of the nagging, unresolved questions.

Justice, peace and the integrity of creation

This is the headline phrase used since 1983 as pointer to the many issues in Christian obedience in the world's life. *Shalom: Biblical Perspectives on Creation, Justice and Peace* by Ulrich Duchrow and G. Liedke (1987) and *Between the Flood and the Rainbow: Interpreting the Conciliar Process of Mutual Commitment* (1992), edited by Preman Niles, introduce the findings of the world convocation at Seoul, Korea, in 1990 and its contribution to many subsequent projects. The 1992 study document *Christian Faith and the World Economy Today* looks further into the economic dimension, Larry Rasmussen's *Earth Community, Earth Ethics* (1996) into the ecological, *Churches in the World of Nations* (1994) by Ninan Koshy into the international/diplomatic, and *Spiritual Values for Earth Community* (2000) by David Hallman into sustainable development, while *Overcoming Violence* by Margot Käsemann (2000) introduces the issues of the Decade to Overcome Violence called by the WCC for 2001-10. Pauline Webb's *A Long Struggle* (1994) chronicles the WCC's contributions over many years to the overthrow of apartheid in South Africa and their successful outcome.

Interfaith dialogue

Again a vast literature. Try *The Bible and People of Other Faiths* (1985) and *Not Without My Neighbour: Issues in Interfaith Relations* (1999), both by Wesley Ariarajah, long the WCC's chief secretary in this field. *My Neighbour's Faith and Mine: Theological Discoveries through Interfaith Dialogue* (1985) is a nine-part study guide for use by local Christian groups. *Salvations: Truth and Difference in Religion* (1995) by Mark Heim, and *The Meaning and End of Religion: A Revolutionary Approach to the Great Religious Traditions* (1962-78) by W. Cantwell Smith are, in their different ways, profound explorations of lasting consequence.

People

A quite different way in to much of the above is to read the stories of some of the people who made it all happen. *Ecumenical Pilgrims: Profiles of Pioneers in Christian Reconciliation* (1995), edited by Ion Bria and Dagmar Heller, offers fifty short biographical studies of persons from many churches and continents. W.A. Visser 't Hooft's *Memoirs* (1973) and Keith Clements' *Faith on the Frontier: A Life of J.H. Oldham* (1999) on the long lives of two of the outstanding leaders are both vividly readable. *Madeleine Barot* by André Jacques (1991) and *Unfinished Agenda* (1985) by Lesslie Newbigin tell of two other deeply loved and influential figures in the first forty years of the WCC.